I0191064

Sir William Cecil: Elizabeth I's Chief Minister

A Tudor Times Insight

By Tudor Times

Published by Tudor Times Ltd

Copyright © 2015 Tudor Times Ltd

The right of Tudor Times Ltd to be identified as the author of the work has been asserted in accordance with the Copyright, Designs and Patents Act 1988.

This book is copyright material and must not be copied, reproduced, transferred, distributed, leased, licensed or publicly performed or used in any way except as specifically permitted in writing by the publishers, as allowed under the terms and conditions under which it was purchased or as strictly permitted by applicable copyright law. Any unauthorised distribution or use of this text may be a direct infringement of the author's and publisher's rights, and those responsible may be liable in law accordingly.

www.tudortimes.co.uk

Tudor Times Insights

Tudor Times Insights are books collating articles from our website www.tudortimes.co.uk which is a repository for a wide variety of information about the Tudor and Stewart period 1485 – 1625. There you can find material on People, Places, Daily Life, Military & Warfare, Politics & Economics and Religion. The site has a Book Review section, with author interviews and a book club. It also features comprehensive family trees, and a 'What's On' event list with information about forthcoming activities relevant to the Tudors and Stewarts.

Titles in the Series

Profiles

Katherine Parr: Henry VIII's Sixth Queen
James IV: King of Scots
Lady Margaret Pole: Countess of Salisbury
Thomas Wolsey: Henry VIII's Cardinal
Marie of Guise: Regent of Scotland
Thomas Cromwell: Henry VIII's Chief Minister
Lady Penelope Devereux: Sir Philip Sidney's Muse
James V: Scotland's Renaissance King
Lady Katherine Grey: Tudor Prisoner
Sir William Cecil: Elizabeth I's Chief Minister
Lady Margaret Douglas: Countess of Lennox
Sir James Melville: Scottish Ambassador
Tudors & Stewarts 2015: A collection of 12 Profiles

People

Who's Who in Wolf Hall

Politics & Economy

Field of Cloth of Gold
Succession: The Tudor Problem
The Pilgrimage of Grace and Exeter Conspiracy

Contents

Sir William Cecil: Elizabeth I's Chief Minister

Introduction

Sir William Cecil, Lord Burghley was the longest-serving and most successful politician of the Tudor age. First as Privy Councillor to Edward VI, and then as Elizabeth I's Secretary and Treasurer, he profoundly influenced the religion and politics of the second half of the sixteenth century. Scourge of the Catholics, and implacable enemy of Mary, Queen of Scots, Cecil's life was devoted to fulfilling his vision of a Protestant nation.

Cecil was a Lincolnshire man, born and bred, and he always saw that county as his own. But as a politician, he needed to keep close to the centre of power and he spent the majority of his life in and around the capital, building several houses to reflect his status.

This book contains Sir William Cecil's Life Story and additional articles about him, looking at different aspects of his life. Whilst politics were central to Cecil's life, he was also a scholar and a bibliophile. Widely read, hungry for knowledge and fascinated by architecture and maps, he took an interest in topics as diverse as gardening, navigation, astronomy and alchemy. Cecil was a family man, close to his parents, siblings and second wife, but not all his personal relationships were successful.

Family Tree

Sir William CECIL
1st Baron Burghley

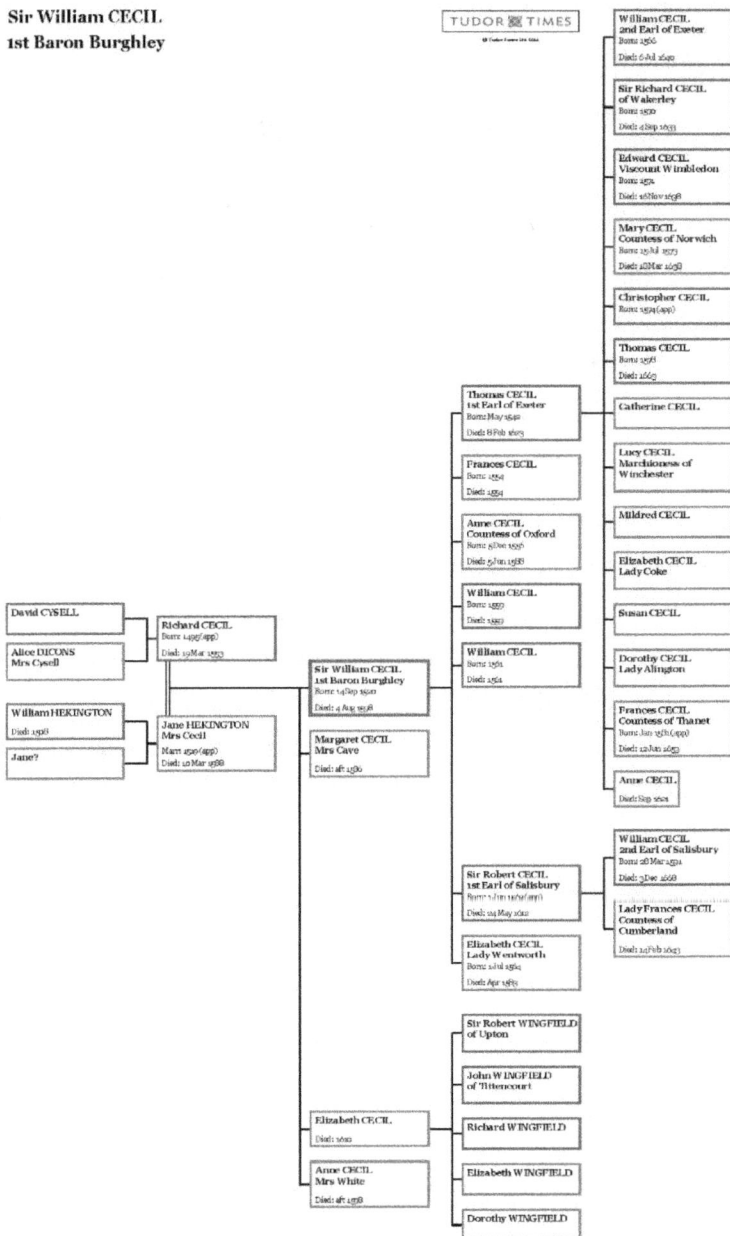

TUDOR TIMES
© Tudor Times Ltd 2016

William CECIL
2nd Earl of Exeter
Born: 1566
Died: 6 Jul 1640

Sir Richard CECIL
of Walcerley
Born: 1570
Died: 28 Sep 1633

Edward CECIL
Viscount Wimbledon
Born: 1572
Died: 16 Nov 1638

Mary CECIL
Countess of Norwich
Born: 29 Jul 1573
Died: 18 Mar 1658

Christopher CECIL
Born: 1574 (app)

Thomas CECIL
Born: 1578
Died: 1663

Thomas CECIL,
1st Earl of Exeter
Born: May 1542
Died: 8 Feb 1623

Catherine CECIL.

Frances CECIL
Born: 1554
Died: 1554

Lucy CECIL,
Marchioness of
Winchester

Anne CECIL,
Countess of Oxford
Born: 5 Dec 1556
Died: 5 Jun 1588

Mildred CECIL.

William CECIL.
Born: 1559
Died: 1559

Elizabeth CECIL,
Lady Coke

David CYSELL

Richard CECIL,
Born: 1496 (app)
Died: 19 Mar 1553

William CECIL.
Born: 1561
Died: 1561

Susan CECIL.

Alice DICONS
Mrs Cysell

Sir William CECIL,
1st Baron Burghley
Born: 14 Sep 1520
Died: 4 Aug 1598

Dorothy CECIL,
Lady Alington

William HEKINGTON
Died: 1506

Jane HEKINGTON
Mrs Cecil
Marr: 1520 (app)
Died: 10 Mar 1588

Frances CECIL,
Countess of Thanet
Born: Jan 1581 (app)
Died: 12 Jun 1653

Jane?

Margaret CECIL,
Mrs Cave
Died: aft 1560

Anne CECIL.
Died: Sep 1602

William CECIL,
2nd Earl of Salisbury
Born: 28 Mar 1591
Died: 3 Dec 1668

Sir Robert CECIL,
1st Earl of Salisbury
Born: 1 Jun 1563 (app)
Died: 24 May 1612

Lady Frances CECIL,
Countess of
Cumberland
Died: 14 Feb 1643

Elizabeth CECIL,
Lady Wentworth
Born: 21 Jul 1564
Died: Apr 1583

Sir Robert WINGFIELD
of Upton

John WINGFIELD
of Tittencourt

Elizabeth CECIL.
Died: 1601

Richard WINGFIELD

Anne CECIL,
Mrs White
Died: aft 1588

Elizabeth WINGFIELD

Dorothy WINGFIELD

Sir William Cecil's Life Story

Chapter 1: Education

Unlike his great predecessors as chief minister to the Tudor monarchs, Morton, Wolsey, and Cromwell, William Cecil probably always looked forward to a career in the royal service. Born in late September 1520 at Bourne in Lincolnshire, his parents were Richard Cecil, a Page in Henry VIII's chamber, and Jane Hekington.

The Hekingtons were amongst the elite of the urban class in Bourne and the nearby town of Stamford. They were town councillors, members of the trade and church guilds and small landowners. The Cecils (or Syssells) had come from Wales only in the latter quarter of the 15th century, but the god-father of Cecil's grandfather, David, one Sir David Philips, held posts under Lady Margaret Beaufort. Lady Margaret's great estate at Collyweston, less than five miles from Stamford made her one of the most important feudal magnates in south Lincolnshire, quite apart from her importance as the mother of King Henry VII.

Cecil thought of Lincolnshire as his 'country' all his life. It was the heart of his family and the enormous estate he created there at Burghley was the patrimony he left to his eldest son. It was also where he chose to be buried. Nevertheless, from an early age, his path took him away from home.

His first steps on the road to royal service were educational. The only boy amongst four siblings, he was sent some 15 miles from home to the King's School at Grantham (the same school later attended by that other illustrious son of Lincolnshire, Sir Isaac Newton). King's School was founded by Henry VII's Lord Privy Seal, Bishop Richard Foxe, also a Lincolnshire man.

The school, which still survives, is in the shadow of the enormous church dedicated to St Wulfram which must have been a focal point for the pupils, whose education was largely aimed at entry to the church or the law. There, Cecil would have practised the religion of his forefathers, surrounded by candles, relics, images of the saints and prayers for the dead.

After a short period at Grantham, Cecil was moved to a school closer to home, the new chantry school at Stamford, where he remained under the supervision of the priest-cum-school master, Libeus Byard, until he was about 14. Then, in 1535, he went to Cambridge. The college he attended, that of St John the Evangelist, again had local connections. It had been founded under the will of Lady Margaret Beaufort by her friend and confessor, John Fisher, Bishop of Rochester. Both Lady Margaret and Fisher were renowned for their piety and their learning, encouraging the Humanist expansion of learning of the late 15th century which became a feature of St John's. Greek, Hebrew and medicine were on the curriculum, in addition to the subjects taught at the other Cambridge Colleges.

When Cecil arrived, he was flung into a maelstrom of political, educational and religious upheaval. The King, Henry VIII, in his quest for an annulment of his marriage to Katharine of Aragon, had rejected the authority of the Pope, an act which Bishop Fisher refused to accept, with fatal consequences. After his execution, which took place in June 1535, about a month after Cecil's arrival, Cromwell sent an order to St John's to have every monument or reference to Fisher defaced.

Whilst Henry had largely intended that the change in overall authority in the church should be the only alteration, the spirit of reform was abroad, and the principles of Luther and other reformers were spreading like wild-fire amongst the intellectuals of the day. St John's College contained a circle of men who would go on to be the first generation of scholars and academics in England who could be termed Protestant.

The group included John Cheke, whose novel approach to the pronunciation of Greek had created waves in traditional academic circles; Roger Ascham, later tutor to the Lady Elizabeth and Lady Jane Grey; and Sir Anthony Denny who had a role in the education of Edward VI. When Cecil arrived, he was drawn to this set and embraced their religious stance, first evangelicalism, concentrating on the importance of the scriptures; then the doctrine of Justification by Faith alone, and finally the rejection of the Mass as predicated on the doctrine of transubstantiation (ie that Christ was really physically present in the bread and wine).

Cecil remained in Cambridge for some five years, leaving in 1540 to complete his education at Gray's Inn in London, where he was admitted to the Bar on 6th May 1541. With strong reformist views, a church career was not on the cards, and a training in civil law was the most obvious home for his talents.

Chapter 2: Councillor in Training

According to Cecil's later reminiscences, he was a member of the Parliament that sat between 16 January 1542 and 28th March 1544, although there is no record of which constituency he represented, nor whether he sat for the whole period or came in on a by-election. This was the Parliament that passed the Third Act of Succession. This Act laid down the order of succession after Henry VIII's son Edward and any child he might have by Katherine Parr, if neither Edward nor such additional children had legitimate heirs. In that case, the crown was to be inherited by Henry's elder daughter, Mary, and her heirs, then, if she had none, his younger daughter, Elizabeth, and her heirs. It also permitted Henry to name, by his will, heirs to follow on from Elizabeth if she had no children. The Act designated as treason any attempt to subvert this arrangement.

During his time in Cambridge, Cecil had become acquainted with John Cheke's sister, Mary, whom he married in August 1541. Her mother, Agnes, was a widow and an established vintner and property owner in Cambridge. She was not, however, of the gentry class, and for this reason (or perhaps the very prompt arrival of their son, Thomas), Cecil's father did not approve of the match. It was unusual for a man of Cecil's class to marry without parental consent, so we might infer that it was a love match, perhaps precipitated by pregnancy. By the end of May 1543, Mary, back in Cambridge, had died, and been buried at her mother's, rather than her husband's expense. For the time being, little Thomas Cecil stayed with Agnes Cheke.

Freed from his hasty marriage (there is no evidence about how he reacted to Mary's death), Cecil was able to make a far more advantageous match. His second wife, whom he married on 21st December 1545 was Mildred Cooke, daughter of the courtier, Anthony Cooke.

The marriage was probably arranged by Cecil's father who would have known Cooke, since the latter was one of the King's 'spears' or bodyguards. Cooke was an exceptionally learned man, and was at the forefront of promoting intellectual education for women. His five daughters, Anne, Mildred, Elizabeth, Margaret and Katherine, learnt Greek and Latin, and both Anne and Mildred became known for their scholarship. Given Cecil's intellectual interests, it seems likely to have been a match to suit both parties. This marriage drew Cecil further into the circle of Reformers and scholars whose influence in the last years of Henry VIII was growing.

This circle included illustrious figures – Queen Katherine Parr, Katherine Willoughby, Dowager Duchess of Suffolk, and Edward Seymour, Earl of Hertford, the King's brother-in-law who all became known to Cecil, and the Duchess of Suffolk remained a lifelong friend. The relationship with Hertford was particularly important as he was likely to be of some importance during the reign of Henry's successor: a time that could not be long in coming. Henry's health was declining as his weight ballooned.

Chapter 3: Somerset's Man

When Henry VIII died in 1547, Hertford became Lord Protector, and Duke of Somerset. By the middle of that year, if not before, Cecil was in his direct employ. Within a year, Cecil had the post of Master of Requests – that is, he had the responsibility of reviewing petitions made to Somerset and sending them on to the appropriate divisions of the Courts at Westminster (not to be confused with the role of Master of the Court of Requests, a legal office).

Despite the fact that Somerset had fallen out with the Queen Dowager, Katherine Parr, Cecil remained on good terms with her. He wrote an effusive introduction to her devotional work, the *Lamentations of a Sinner*, which he registered for her at Stationer's Hall in late 1547. This friendship with her step-mother may have been the root of Elizabeth and Cecil's acquaintanceship.

In the political world of the sixteenth century, a system of favours and place-seeking for friends and family that we would consider corrupt, was the norm. The mediaeval concept of '*good-lordship*' whereby the lower ranking person (both men and women) gave service, or gifts in return for the higher-ranking individual putting them forward for plum jobs continued, although, as the century progressed, it began to be questioned. Cecil was now in a position to do favours for people, and he began to be seen as a man of influence.

One of Somerset's pet projects was the forcible absorption of Scotland into English domination. The project had been begun by Henry VIII, when his nephew, James V, died, leaving a week old baby as queen. Henry had leapt at the idea of marrying her to his son, Edward. The Scottish Regent, Arran, initially in favour, could not force the scheme through his Parliament, and the little Queen Mary was hidden away from the risk of abduction by her terrifying great-uncle. Henry, with Somerset as his lieutenant, had made war on the recalcitrant Scots. Somerset, a notable soldier, continued the policy, and led an army north in person.

Cecil was part of this force, not, officially as a soldier, but as a judge of the Court of the Verge. This court was responsible for jurisdiction in disputes involving members of the sovereign's court that took place within a 12-mile radius of wherever the sovereign happened to be. Presumably it was considered likely that there would be disputes between men on campaign. Whilst away, Cecil and his colleague, William Patten, kept journals. Patten used their memoranda to write his book 'The Expedition into Scotland' published in 1548. The expedition was, from the English perspective, extremely successful, culminating on 10th September 1547 with the Battle of Pinkie Cleugh, which effectively annihilated Scotland's army, and allowed the English, including Cecil, to burn Leith and besiege Edinburgh.

This vision of incorporating the neighbouring kingdom into a single, Protestant, country of Britain, followed Cecil throughout his life, and much of his later policy as Elizabeth's chief minister, was undertaken with the goal of achieving it.

Somerset's rule also introduced extensive religious reforms, which Cecil wholeheartedly supported. Change began to be visible in churches in the summer of 1547, when, as well as reinforcing the requirement for an English Bible and a copy of Erasmus' *Paraphrases* to be in every parish church, the incumbents were exhorted to remove anything that could tend to idolatry or image worship. The statues of the saints and the holy relics which had been objects of veneration for hundreds of years began to be removed, although wholesale destruction did not happen until after the passing of the Chantries Act of 1548.

This Act disbanded the religious guilds that had been such an important feature of mediaeval life: that mixture of civic duty and religious devotion that had built the churches and cathedrals, and instituted a whole system based on belief in the doctrine of purgatory. Now, prayers for the dead were outlawed, the chantries which had been endowed for priests to say Masses for souls for the dead were torn down, and a wave of window-smashing, and destruction of images rolled over the country.

The chantries had been staffed by priests who, when they were not saying the obligatory Masses (a priest could only offer two per day), frequently taught the local children. In just such a chantry school at Stamford had Cecil received his own education. Now, although Cecil was committed to reform, he used his influence to have a private act passed re-founding his old school as a Grammar School, affiliated to St John's College, Cambridge and under the mastership of his old teacher, Libeus Byard.

Not everyone was happy with these religious changes. In particular, Stephen Gardiner, Bishop of Winchester, who had led the conservative faction in Henry VIII's last years, objected strongly to religious changes being made before Edward VI reached his majority. Cecil was sent by Somerset to try to persuade Gardiner to conform to government policy, but met with no success. Gardiner preached a very public sermon, condemning the changes.

Then came the 1549 Book of Common Prayer. Probably the work of Thomas Cranmer, Archbishop of Canterbury, it changed church services from Latin to English, and reduced and changed some of the ceremony and ritual. It was based on the traditional Sarum rite of the English Church, and its central ceremony of the Eucharist was ambiguously worded, allowing for both Catholic and Protestant interpretation. Nevertheless, for the more conservatively minded (which was the vast majority of people outside London and East Anglia, where Protestantism flourished), it was unacceptable. Cornwall rose in revolt - in the Prayer Book Rebellion.

Almost simultaneously, in the east of the country, there was a rebellion motivated by economic factors, led by Robert Kett, eventually put down by John Dudley, Earl of Warwick.

Somerset's inability to control events and his high-handed attitude to his colleagues on the Council had lost him popularity, and in the autumn of 1549 he was relieved of office. His friends and colleagues also suffered, and on 24th November 1549, William Cecil was dispatched to the Tower of London.

Chapter 4: Working with Northumberland

Cecil spent eight weeks in the Tower, although comfortably housed, and not subject to any mistreatment. He was released on 25th January 1550, to find that the new man in charge was Dudley, Earl of Warwick. Over the following year the power struggle between Somerset and Warwick continued. Cecil, reading the writing on the wall, abandoned his old master and began to work with Warwick.

On 5th September 1550, in a ceremony at Oatlands Palace, Cecil was given a place on the Privy Council as Secretary to the King. This was an important position, giving access to the monarch, and involving Cecil in all state business. He shared the office with Sir William Petre. Cecil also continued to work with in a more direct capacity for Warwick as his secretary.

As the impetus for Protestant reformation grew, the Privy Council became increasingly concerned about the non-compliance of the Lady Mary, the King's half-sister and heir, to the 1549 Act of Uniformity. Mary refused to countenance any changes to the services laid down in the time of her father, on the stated grounds that, during the King's minority, the Council had no power to change religion. It was widely known, however, that her objections were religious, rather than political. A number of attempts to force her to conform, by imprisoning her household officers, had failed. Mary remained intransigent.

In August 1551, Mary received a letter in the King's name. She received it very properly, kneeling and kissing the seal. But Mary had a sarcastic turn of phrase, and as she read it, she commented aloud:

'*Ah, good Master Cecil took much pain here.*'

Mary's powerful cousin, the Emperor Charles V, intervened and secured permission for her to hear the traditional Mass, privately. Mary flagrantly abused this privilege, inviting all and sundry to her chapel, but the English government was not in a position to take action. Nevertheless, the drive for reform continued, and Cecil hosted a debate at his house in Canon's Row, Westminster, during which five scholars, including Cecil himself, debated against the doctrine of transubstantiation (that Christ was really, physically, present in the bread and wine). Two men argued in favour of this Catholic interpretation.

Soon after this, on 11th October, 1551, Cecil was knighted in a ceremony at Hampton Court. This was also the occasion for Warwick to be promoted to Duke of Northumberland, making him of equal rank with Somerset, and Henry Grey, Marquess of Dorset and the new Duke's crony, to the Duchy of Suffolk. Tensions between Northumberland and Somerset continued. Cecil seems to have had little hesitation in supporting his new master, and, when Somerset was executed in January 1552, there were no repercussions for his erstwhile friend.

In August 1552, the powerful Scottish preacher, John Knox, arrived at the English Court, taken by Northumberland, who had heard him preach in Newcastle and appointed him as his chaplain. Cecil and Knox seem to have developed, if not a friendship, then at least a position of mutual respect. Knox was at the radical end of Protestantism. He preached in front of Edward VI and Cranmer, Archbishop of Canterbury. What he had to say shook the court. Cranmer, persuaded by the types of argument and debate that Cecil had hosted, had revised the 1549 Prayer Book into a more Protestant version, clearly denying transubstantiation, but commanding Communicants to kneel as a sign of respect. Knox claimed this was idolatry, infuriating the Archbishop. Cranmer became even more enraged when a body of evangelical preachers was engaged by the Privy Council to review his Prayer Book – this included Knox.

Knox was invited to become Bishop of Rochester, but refused. Northumberland wrote to Cecil, explaining that, if Knox could be persuaded to accept, he would firstly, keep Cranmer on his toes, and secondly, stop preaching excessively radical doctrines in the North, and attracting crowds of Scots from over the border. Knox discussed the matter with Cecil, telling him that he would decline the bishopric.

Cecil refused to be Knox's messenger, telling him would have to break the bad news personally. Northumberland was disgruntled, and told Cecil that

'[he loved] not to have to do with men which be neither grateful nor pleasable...'

Cecil continued to correspond with Knox, and it is likely that Knox's views on the necessity for reform in Scotland (still officially Catholic, and ruled by the Queen Dowager, Marie of Guise, as Regent for Mary, Queen of Scots, who was in France) influenced his views on Anglo-Scottish policy.

Cecil was also, perhaps, influenced by Knox's announcement in January 1553, that there were secret traitors, just waiting for Edward VI to die, so that they could bring back Catholicism. Certainly, there were others who believed that for Mary to succeed would spell disaster, and so was born the scheme to change the succession from that laid down in the Act of Succession 1544.

Chapter 5: The 1553 Succession Crisis

In early 1553, Edward VI drew up a *'Devise for the Succession'* which attempted to overturn the Act of Succession 1544. The King's initial plan had been to find a male, Protestant, successor (overlooking the male, Catholic, Lord Darnley, and his own half-sisters). But by June, Edward's time was running out and there was no time for more boys to be born. He settled the succession on his evangelically Protestant cousin, Lady Jane Grey.

The level to which Edward was influenced by Northumberland has been a matter of some debate. There can be little doubt that Edward wanted to preserve his Protestant reformation, and that he would prefer to be succeeded by Lady Jane than by his sister Mary. Equally, Northumberland would benefit as he was Lady Jane's father-in-law. Cecil's level of involvement is also difficult to pin down precisely. We might infer that he would have preferred the crown to pass to Jane – they were of similar mind in religious matters. There was also a family connection – Jane's cousin, Frances Grey of Pirgo, was married to Cecil's brother-in-law, William Cooke. That may seem a rather distant connection today, but, in the sixteenth century, the extended family was an important network of influence.

There is no evidence of Cecil's state of mind, and the detailed record of his actions is contained in the exculpatory letters he sent to Queen Mary after the event, so we might suppose he gave himself the benefit of the doubt when telling her his story.

In spring of 1553, Cecil was absent from court – his father had died, and he himself had taken to his bed with an illness that lasted for nearly two months. On his return in May, he discovered that the King had no hope of surviving the summer and that there was a plan to subvert the succession. He avoided Privy Council meetings, so as not to be involved. Fearing trouble, he arranged for his money and valuables to be hidden.

On 11th June, he was obliged to attend a Council meeting, at which Lord Chief Justice Montague had been invited by the Privy Councillors (including Cecil himself) to attend to give evidence as to the legality of changing the succession without an Act of Parliament. King Edward told Montague he wanted his '*Devise*' implemented, but Montague informed King and Council that to implement it would be treason, as defined by the Act of 1544. The King's personal Devise could not trump an Act of Parliament. This was never going to be music to a Tudor king's ears – even one so young as Edward. Montague was ordered to do as he was told and draw the Devise into legal form. He resisted as long as he could, trying to persuade Edward to call Parliament to make the changes required.

The King was not willing to wait, so, bullied and threatened with dire consequences by King and Council, Montague drew up the document, first requesting a pardon under the Great Seal. In the background, Cecil shared his misgivings with some of his friends and family – including his wife's brother-in-law, Nicholas Bacon. Bacon's wife, Anne Cooke, was a close friend of the Lady Mary's, so it was politic to get his doubts into the right ears.

Once the legal document was drawn up, Cecil, like all the others, added his signature. He claimed however, that he signed only as a witness of the King's intention. No doubt he, like all of his colleagues, was praying for the King to live long enough for the Parliament that had been summoned to relieve him of the taint of treason which clung about them all.

Edward, however, did not live long enough. He died on 6th July 1553, and Cecil was now faced with the choice of committing active treason by supporting Lady Jane, or not. Jane's new Privy Council wrote an offensive letter to Mary, pointing out that as she was illegitimate she could not inherit. Cecil, although he declined to write the offending missive, signed it. He also avoided writing any other letters that were blatantly treasonable, such as orders to the Lords Lieutenant of the counties, or Jane's Accession Proclamation. He did, however, take the oath of fealty to Jane.

Cecil then began (or so he later claimed) to actively undermine Jane's authority. He sounded out his fellow Secretary, Sir William Petre, the Earls of Winchester, Bedford and Arundel and Lord Darcy, with a view to handing over Windsor Castle to Mary. Whether this counter-coup was real, or would have been successful, became, in the end, a moot point. Mary was victorious, and by early August was on her way to London to claim her crown, and to meet a Privy Council, including Cecil, that had suddenly discovered that it had supported her all along.

Cecil raced to meet her, sending his servant, Robert Alford, in advance, and travelling with Nicholas Bacon. He also composed a detailed defence of his actions. He finally came into Mary's presence on 31st July at Ingatestone Hall.

Whether Mary believed his protestations is debatable. However, her policy from the beginning was to accept the grovelling from the councillors, and let them pin all of the blame on Northumberland and his two closest allies.

Cecil's last act as Secretary to Edward VI was to march in his funeral procession on 8th August, 1553.

Chapter 6: Mary's Reign

Cecil was not immediately reappointed to public office as some of his former colleagues, such as Paget and the Earl of Winchester were. He retired to his house at Wimbledon with his family, and, to public view, lived quietly. It seems, however, from evidence presented by his biographer, Stephen Alford, that he was giving support to men undermining the new government. In particular, he hoped to mke life difficult for his old adversary, Gardiner, Bishop of Winchester, now, having been released from the Tower, Lord Chancellor.

A man named Day, working at least in part with Cecil's brother-in-law, William Cooke, was running a secret printing press from land owned by Cecil in Lincolnshire. The works he printed attacked the new government's stance on religion and produced hagiographical works about Lady Jane.

On religious matters, Cecil conformed. Other Protestants were not willing to bow to the restoration of the old faith and went into exile. These exiles included Cecil's friend, Katherine Willoughby, Dowager Duchess of Suffolk and her new husband, Richard Bertie, as well as Cecil's father-in-law, Sir Anthony Cooke. Others stayed home. Sir Nicholas Bacon remained in his post at the Court of Wards and Liveries, with his wife now a Gentlewoman of the Privy Chamber. Roger Ascham,

Cecil's old friend from Cambridge, was the new Queen's Latin Secretary. Sooner or later, it seemed likely that Cecil would return to office.

In the meanwhile, Cecil retained a connection with the Queen's sister, and, for the time being, heir, Elizabeth. He had become steward of some of her lands in Lincolnshire, early in the reign of Edward, and continued in that post.

Cecil's chance at rehabilitation came in 1554 when he was commanded to act as host to one of the Secretaries of Philip of Spain, who had arrived in England and married the Queen in July 1554. He then gained a further step when, with what might have been an exquisite sense of irony on the part of Queen Mary, Cecil was sent to Brussels to greet Reginald, Cardinal Pole and escort him back to England after an exile of nearly thirty years.

Pole was returning to England to take up the position of Archbishop of Canterbury, and to return the country to the Roman fold. Surprisingly, Pole and Cecil got on well. Pole (who was later traduced as a heretic by the Pope himself, for his reforming stance) wanted to reform Catholicism in many of the ways that had been first mooted, back in the 1520s, and the scholar in both men appreciated the other.

In early 1555, it looked as though Mary would have a child, reinforcing the return to Rome, and, from Cecil's perspective, the best thing to do was to accept reality and make the most of the new situation. He continued to build links with Mary's Privy Council, and even sent her a gift. Slow integration continued, and in 1555 he was part of a delegation that travelled to Brussels to treat of peace between France and Spain. He then spent a couple of months travelling.

Cecil was returned to Parliament in 1555, where he was one of the opponents of a government bill to confiscate the lands of the Protestant exiles. It was a subject to touch him closely, with many of his friends abroad. The bill was defeated when the opponents locked the supporters out of the House and forced a count. The government was not happy with this misconduct by the Commons, but took no action, beyond sending stern reprimands.

Cecil had purchased the lease of the Rectory of Wimbledon back in 1549. The Manor of Wimbledon (Crown land) was now granted to Pole, and Cecil lobbied hard to become his steward for the land, a position granted in 1556. The Cecils continued to show public conformity to Catholicism. Mildred attended one of Pole's great public sermons, and the couple attended Mass in St Mary's Church, Wimbledon at Easter 1556. As he was 'rector' of the parish, the offerings from the Easter Mass, less the costs of bread, wine, candles etc went into his pocket.

Meanwhile, those who would make no outward show of conformity were punished with increasing severity – nearly three hundred people, some of whom were Cecil's former colleagues, such as Cranmer, and the Bishops Latimer and Ridley, were burnt. Sir John Cheke, his brother-in-law, although he had initially deplored those who hid their Protestant beliefs, was offered the choice of recantation, or burning. He chose the former.

During these years, the Cecils visited their friends and family, waited on their patrons at court, and began a family. Their first child, Frances, born in 1554, lived only a few hours, but their second, Anne, born in 1556, survived. They attended christenings and weddings, frequently amongst Mildred's Cooke, Bacon, Grey and Hoby connections. Cecil was also continuing to make himself useful to Mary's Councillors and visiting Cardinal Pole.

Things began to change in 1558. The loss of Calais weighed heavily on the Queen and her government, and Mary's renewed hope of pregnancy was not widely believed to have firm foundations. Her health was failing, and the prospect of Elizabeth becoming Queen became closer. During February 1558, Cecil paid a visit to Elizabeth, ostensibly, no doubt to discuss his stewardship of her lands, but perhaps with other intentions, too. By October, it was only a matter of time before Elizabeth became Queen. King Philip's Ambassador, Count Feria, wrote to the King, noting that it was likely that Cecil would be appointed to her government. He described Cecil as:

'...said to be an able and virtuous man but a heretic.'

On 17th November, 1558, both Queen Mary and Cardinal Pole died of influenza. Cecil was at Hatfield on that day, with Elizabeth, and they were already planning for the future.

Chapter 7: Urgent Problems

On 20th November, 1558, Cecil was sworn to Elizabeth's Privy Council, and took the office of Master Secretary. In addition to the usual oath of office, it is recorded that Elizabeth gave the great charge of his office to Cecil with the following words:

'This judgement I have of you, that you will not be corrupted with any manner of gift and that you will be faithful to the state, and that without respect of my private will you will give me that counsel that you think best. And if you know anything necessary to be declared to me of secrecy, you shall show it to myself only, and assure yourself I shall keep taciturnity therein, and therefore herewith I charge you.'

Their political partnership was to last for forty years – not without differences in many areas of policy, but ultimately in the forging of a nation state that truly brought England from the middle ages, to the discernible parent of the United Kingdom of the twenty-first century.

On Elizabeth's succession there were four major problems facing her government: the war with France, the rebellion in neighbouring

Scotland, religion and the succession. Cecil had decided views on all of these, generally more radical than Elizabeth's.

First, there was the ongoing war. England was Spain's ally in the ongoing round of the interminable Franco-Spanish war that had begun in the 1490s. Although the current outbreak had brought initial success for them, at the Battle of St Quentin in 1557, this had been followed up by the loss of Calais and the decided coolness of Spanish efforts to help recapture it. France and Spain finally made a lasting peace at the Treaty of Cateau-Cambresis, and, although whilst Mary lived, her husband, Philip II tried to include the return of Calais as part of the deal, once he was no longer King of England, he had less interest in pursuing it. England was in no financial position to prosecute the war alone, and had little option but to join in the treaty as agreed. Cecil saw this as evidence of the Catholic powers putting their differences aside to isolate Protestant England.

The nightmare scenario he envisaged was the use of Scotland by France as a back-door into England. The King of France's daughter-in-law was Queen of Scots, and, in the opinion of Catholic Europe was the rightful Queen of England, following Mary I's death. Now it was no longer preoccupied with Spain, France would invade on two fronts.

The solution to this, in Cecil's view, would be for England to support the Lords of the Congregation. This was a group of Scots nobles who, largely under the influence of John Knox, had converted to Protestantism, and who were no longer as convinced as they had been in the 1540s that France was a friend, and England an enemy. The Lords rejected the authority of the Queen Regent, Marie of Guise, who had called for French troops to regain control. Cecil was in constant communication with the Lords and was certain that England should send money and men to help them.

Unfortunately, he was having trouble persuading Elizabeth of the merits of supporting rebellious subjects. Throughout her reign Elizabeth hesitated to support rebels against their lawful prince. For her, solidarity amongst monarchs was more important than solidarity with her co-religionists, especially as the more vocal Protestants like Knox had far more extreme religious beliefs than hers. For Cecil however, the opposite was true. He believed, and would continue to try to persuade the Queen, that England should support Protestant rebels against their Catholic masters.

In 1559, John Knox sought a safe conduct to travel through England. Elizabeth trenchantly refused. Not only was he encouraging rebellion, he was also undermining her own position as Queen with his diatribes against women rulers. Knox had loudly criticised Marie, and also the late Mary I, in his '*First Blast of the Trumpet against the Monstrous Regiment of Women*' excoriating female rule.

The offensive language of the '*First Blast...*' was an affront to Elizabeth. Every attempt of Knox to dig himself out of the hole he had created by claiming that he had not meant to offend her failed. He did suggest that, provided she admitted that she was an exception, with a special dispensation from God from His usual laws against women rulers, then no-one would be happier to maintain her authority than himself. On the other hand, if she believed that she was Queen because of custom and law, '*her ingratitude [would] not long lack punishment.*'

He asked Cecil to share his views with Elizabeth. One can only imagine Cecil's reaction to such inflammatory language. He declined to answer Knox and certainly didn't communicate his views to Elizabeth. Nevertheless, Cecil was determined to help the Scots Lords and under his control, the Privy Council wrote encouraging words, but there was still Elizabeth to persuade.

Then the Queen of Scots committed what, with hindsight, was probably the greatest mistake of her life. Only sixteen, newly married and crowned as Queen of France (Henri II having died in July 1559), she accepted the Catholic, French view that, in law, if not in fact, she, Mary, was the rightful Queen of England. She quartered her arms with those of England and she and her husband called themselves Kings of France, Scotland and England. For Cecil, this was proof positive that Mary was Elizabeth's bitter enemy, and, for the rest of Mary's life, he sought every possible means to undermine her, and eventually, dispatch her.

Elizabeth, not yet secure on her throne, although furious at Mary's action, still had to be persuaded to act. Initially, Cecil failed to induce his colleagues on the Council to do more than make encouraging noises: not even his brother-in-law, Nicholas Bacon was convinced. It was not until they heard that a French fleet had put to sea in support of the Scottish Regent that the whole Council recommended to Elizabeth that she support the Lords. The Queen, however, rejected their advice out-of-hand. It was only in February 1560, after months of argument, that Elizabeth agreed to give the Lords military assistance.

Cecil travelled north to Edinburgh, where he agreed the Treaty of Edinburgh with the Lords. From the point of view of Cecil and the English, the Treaty was a triumph. From the perspective of the legitimate government of Scotland, Queen Mary and her husband, it was quite unacceptable. The Treaty provided that, if Mary failed to ratify its terms, the English would be free militarily to protect the Protestant religion in Scotland, and prevent French intervention. It also acknowledged Elizabeth as the legitimate Queen of England. Mary never ratified the treaty, but the clauses relating to the withdrawal of French troops were fulfilled.

Chapter 8: The Religious Settlement

Whilst the vast majority of the populace outside London and the South East were largely Catholic in their habits and customs, Elizabeth's immediate advisors were generally Protestant, and many had either been exiles from Mary's rule or had been hiding their religion under a cloak of conformity and were now eager to continue the Protestant reformation begun in Edward's reign.   This prevalence of Protestants in her government, led by Cecil, together with a growing dislike of religious persecution (although we need to be careful not to read contemporary reaction solely through the eyes of the martyrologist and vehement Protestant John Foxe) meant a break with Rome was inevitable.

The Pope, Paul IV, not certain of Elizabeth's views, and an inveterate enemy of Spain, was hopeful that she might prove a more biddable member of his flock than Mary had, but he was doomed to disappointment.   Whilst Elizabeth never discussed her legitimacy or otherwise, it would be hard for her to accept the Roman Catholic position on her parents' marriage - that it was bigamous and unlawful.

Prior to the meeting of her first Parliament, the law was observed at Elizabeth's court and elsewhere, and the Catholic Mass continued, although Elizabeth showed her rejection of transubstantiation by walking out of Chapel when the priest elevated the Host.   Nevertheless, her religious preferences were conservative, and her preferred resolution would have been the reinstitution of the ambiguous 1549 Book of Common Prayer, with acceptance of the monarch, rather than the Pope, as Supreme Head of the Church in England.

A bill to restore Church supremacy to the monarch was introduced in Elizabeth's first Parliament. Guided by Cecil's father-in-law, Anthony Cooke, newly returned from exile, and his brother-in-law, Nicholas Bacon, it eventually passed through the Commons, although not easily. It went to the Lords, where there was strong opposition from both peers and bishops. The Archbishop of York (the senior ecclesiastic, as the see of Canterbury was vacant) pointed out that as a woman could not be a priest, she could not possibly be the head of the Church. The arguments continued, and, instead of the quick return to the Protestant regime of Edward, Cecil found himself stymied.

As the Lords and Bishops could not be punished for their speeches in Parliament, he came up with a scheme to trap the Bishops into appearing to disobey an order from Elizabeth's Council during a debate elsewhere on religion. A couple of the most recalcitrant were sent to the Tower and the others given the opportunity to rethink their objections when a new Supremacy Bill came forward. Again, the Lords were divided, but although all of the Bishops rejected it, the absence of two of them in the Tower, and the strange non-appearance of Dr Feckenham, the Abbot of Westminster, who had led the calls for refusal, meant that the bill was carried by three votes.

The law of the land, enshrined in the Act of Uniformity 1559 now stated that all ministers (not priests) of the Church of England must use the 1559 Prayer Book, which mirrored the 1552 book, amended by deletion of some statements highly offensive to Catholics about the Bishop of Rome, and removal also of the clear statement that the bread and wine do not change.

To encourage consistency and acceptance of the new rules, every person was to attend the parish church and hear the prescribed service each Sunday, on pain of a fine of 1s. Gentlemen who had their own chapels were exempted, a proviso that saved the position of many of the Catholic nobles, who continued to hear Mass privately. The programme of education of the laity and reform of the clergy which had been part of Mary and Cardinal Pole's plan continued, but with a Protestant bent. In particular, clergy were permitted to marry, something Elizabeth heartily disliked. It was all Cecil could do to persuade her to accept it and, throughout her life she would either ignore, or be rude to, clerical wives. Where he had no success was in the matter of candles and flowers in the Queen's own chapel.

Chapter 9: The Succession

The issue that consumed a vast proportion of Cecil's time in the 1560s was that perennial Tudor favourite, the succession. In accordance with the powers granted in the 1544 Act of Succession, in his Will, Henry VIII had nominated the heirs of the Lady Frances to succeed. With her eldest daughter, Lady Jane Grey now dead, this right devolved on her second daughter, Lady Katherine Grey.

Although there can be no doubt whatsoever that Cecil wanted Elizabeth as queen, and for her to marry and bear an heir, he was quite content with the notion of Lady Katherine as a successor. She was a family connection, and presumably a Protestant, although she had never been as ardent as her sister and had cheerfully conformed under Mary. Mary had treated the Greys kindly, but had made it pretty clear that her personal choice, lacking an heir of her body, would be another cousin, Lady Margaret Douglas, Countess of Lennox, a good Catholic, with a son.

Elizabeth cordially disliked the Grey sisters, and demoted Lady Katherine from her position in the Privy Chamber. She disliked Lady Lennox even more, but was content to play her various cousins off against each other. Elizabeth abhorred any mention of the topic of the succession and never, in all her long life, made an unambiguous statement about it. However, we can infer from some of her comments that she believed her legitimate heir was Mary of Scotland, a view probably shared at the beginning of her reign with her largely Catholic nobles, none of whom wanted interference with the usual laws of inheritance.

For Cecil and the Protestants, however, the idea of Mary of Scotland as queen was their worst nightmare. All of their energies therefore went into persuading Elizabeth herself to marry as soon as possible. Writing to Sir Nicholas Throckmorton, England's Ambassador to France, Cecil said:

'God send our mistress a husband and by him a son, that we may have a masculine succession.'

Elizabeth never rejected the concept totally. Whilst we can look back and consider that her eventual non-marriage worked well, it is not clear that that was a conscious decision by the Queen herself. It was more that the right candidate never appeared. The princes of Europe were generally Catholic, and the example of the trouble caused by her predecessor's choice of a foreign king didn't seem to make that a good idea.

But marriage to one of her own subjects was also fraught with difficulty. The Scottish Earl of Arran, heir in 1560 to Mary, Queen of Scots until she remarried and had a child, suggested his own son, but Elizabeth didn't care much for that idea – fortunately, as the gentleman in question went mad in 1562 and spent the rest of his life in confinement.

Elizabeth's own closest male heir was the young Lord Darnley, son of Lady Lennox, but in 1560 he was only fourteen. The next male heir was Henry Hastings, Earl of Huntingdon, descendant of both the Duke of Buckingham, executed in 1521, and Margaret, Countess of Salisbury, executed in 1541. He was Protestant, even Puritan, but he was already married to Katherine Dudley, daughter of the late Duke of Northumberland.

Cecil and the Privy Council sought out candidates everywhere, but they were hampered not just by the lack of choice but by Elizabeth's own feelings. During the early 1560s it was apparent to every on-looker that

Elizabeth was deeply in love with her Master of Horse, Lord Robert Dudley. He was constantly at her side. They danced, hunted, gambled and laughed together.

Fortunately, from the perspective of Cecil, Dudley was not free to marry. His long-suffering wife was stuck in the country whilst Lord Robert sat up till all hours flirting with the Queen. Nevertheless, Cecil was horrified by the Queen's imprudent behaviour and pleaded with her to moderate her public conduct, especially when foreign rulers, who were still considering marriage treaties, began to suspect that the Queen was sleeping with Dudley – a charge she always denied.

Matters came to a head in September 1560 when Cecil told the Spanish Ambassador that he was so appalled by Elizabeth's behaviour that he was planning to resign, especially, said Cecil, as Elizabeth and Dudley were planning to kill Lady Dudley. It seems quite astonishing that the cautious Cecil would have said such a thing to a foreign ambassador, had he not had an ulterior motive, particularly as, within days, Lady Dudley was indeed dead in suspicious circumstances. Whatever Cecil's motivation for his bizarre comments, the result of events was that Elizabeth could never marry a man whose wife was rumoured to have been murdered – that threat, at least, was over, although Dudley did not cease to hope for another fifteen years.

But, as if Elizabeth's headstrong behaviour were not enough, Cecil's own preferred candidate for her successor, Lady Katherine Grey, had called forth the Queen's wrath by a secret marriage and pregnancy. Cecil was quite unable to deflect Elizabeth's wrath from the offending girl, who was sent to the Tower.

In 1563, the House of Commons, at the suggestion of the Privy Council, brought forth a petition to the Queen, requesting her to name her successor. Elizabeth listened politely, then, saying it was an important matter, which required much thought, agreed to consider the request. The Lords then followed suit, receiving the same answer. This was not good enough for Cecil, who drafted articles for a bill to deal with the disaster of Elizabeth's death. Instead of the Crown passing automatically to her heir (whether that were considered to be Mary of Scotland or Lady Katherine Grey), regal authority would pass to a Privy Council of twenty-four until such time as Parliament selected an appropriate, Protestant, monarch.

Not surprisingly, this draft bill failed to receive any support from Elizabeth. She would not be forced by Parliament, the Privy Council, Cecil or anyone else to derogate from the principle that monarchs rule by God-given right, not through appointment by Parliament.

Cecil's efforts to persuade Elizabeth to name a successor rumbled on, without success, at least until after the death of Mary, Queen of Scots in 1587. By then, her obvious heir was Mary's son, James, who, as a Protestant, would be able to fulfil Cecil's dream of a single, British, Protestant state, although Cecil did not live to see it.

Chapter 10: Marriage Negotiations

The only cure for the succession problem, in Cecil's eyes, was marriage for Elizabeth. Throughout the 1560s and 1570s, he continued to press her to choose a husband. Her first suitor had been Philip of Spain, widower of Queen Mary, but he soon gave up pursuit, marrying Elisabeth de Valois as part of the Treaty of Cateau-Cambresis. Although Cecil would have disliked his Catholicism, he was, at least a known quantity.

Then there was Philip's cousin (and nephew), the Archduke Charles, son of Emperor Ferdinand I. Archduke Charles, also being touted for Mary, Queen of Scots, was the front-runner in the period 1564 – 1568 (early negotiations in 1560 having collapsed). Whilst he was Catholic, the Imperial Hapsburgs were more emollient on religious matters than the Spanish branch of the family and Cecil re-opened negotiations in 1565. The Austrians, however, were wary, after the previous failure.

There was another Charles in the frame, too. Charles IX of France was promoted by his mother, the Queen Regent, Catherine de Medici. His age (he was only fourteen) was rather a drawback, as Elizabeth was now thirty. He was also described as *'pale and not greatly timbered (skinny)'*. She firmly rejected the unappealing prospect of marriage to a teenager, and decided that the Archduke was her favourite choice. She had heard how happy the Archduke Charles' parents had been, and was confident he would be a loving husband. She could not, however, marry him sight unseen – would he visit her?

At this point, the Imperial Ambassador began to smell a rat, and wrote home that:

'She was determined not to marry and therefore found none who pleased her...'

Meanwhile, Mary of Scotland had married Lord Darnley, to the consternation of all of Elizabeth's advisors – the merging of their two claims to the English Crown, and the likelihood that Mary would have a child seemed to increase the threat to their unmarried queen. Elizabeth, overcome by stress, gave way to an emotional outburst, screaming at Cecil, Dudley and others that their pressure on her to marry would ruin her.

Cecil reassured her that they were her loyal subjects, and would never try to force her against her will, but, regardless of his gentle words, the pressure continued, with further petitions from Parliament.

In 1567, the match with Archduke Charles was finally abandoned when a religious compromise in which he would be permitted to hear

Mass in private, provided he also attended the Protestant service with the Queen, did not garner sufficient support in the Privy Council.

By 1570, it appeared that Elizabeth was regretting her failure to marry and secure an heir. In that year, following the Rising of the Northern Earls, in support of Mary, Queen of Scots' succession to the throne, the Pope had finally excommunicated Elizabeth and released Catholics from their duty of obedience to their monarch. In the face of this massively increased threat to her security, Elizabeth needed allies and told the French Ambassador that she intended to marry, not because she wanted to, but to satisfy her subjects. Even Cecil was convinced by her change of heart, writing:

'If I be not much deceived, her Majesty is earnest in this.'

She turned to France for a possible mate. Having rejected Charles IX on the score of the disparity in their ages, she now looked to his younger brother, Henri, even younger, and rumoured throughout Europe to be bisexual (although that term was not used). Initially, Henri was unenthusiastic, and made extremely ungallant remarks about his intended bride, but was talked round by his mother, Catherine de Medici. His religion, however, was the bugbear. Again, an arrangement whereby he could hear Mass privately, if he accompanied Elizabeth to chapel, was mooted. Cecil, although he hated Catholics, and the French in equal measure, wrote to Sir Francis Walsingham, English Ambassador in Paris that:

'I see the imminent perils to this state... that I cannot but persist in seeking marriage for her Majesty.'

But it was not to be. Elizabeth still dithered, and Henri soon reverted to his original refusal.

The final contender for Elizabeth's hand, and the man whom she perhaps might have married, was the younger brother of Charles IX and

Henri. This was François, Duke of Anjou. Although Catholic, he had been instrumental in achieving tolerance for the Huguenots in France, so might be persuadable on religious matters. He had also been active in the Low Countries on the side of the rebels against Spain, which would play well with those of Elizabeth's advisors, including Cecil, who wanted her to intervene there. If Anjou could lead troops there on behalf of England, rather than France, that would be a great strategic advantage. Cecil, together with the Earl of Sussex, supported the match, whilst Dudley (now Earl of Leicester) and Walsingham opposed it.

Negotiations continued, and Anjou sent his envoy, Jean de Simier, to England to woo Elizabeth on his behalf, with a level of success that horrified the opponents of the match, particularly Leicester. Eventually, Anjou even came himself, and he and Elizabeth became surprisingly close.

After all the urging to Elizabeth to marry that had been going on for twenty years, when it looked as though she was finally about to take the plunge, her advisers and the public began to back-track.

Cecil wrote one of his lists of pros and cons – in favour was the fact that, despite being forty-five, Elizabeth was in good health, and would still be able to bear a child. Against the proposition, he noted that she '*misliked*' the idea of marriage.

A tract criticising the marriage, snappily called '*The Discovery of a Gaping Gulf wherein England is like to be swallowed by another French marriage if the Lord forbid not the banns by letting Her Majesty see the sin and punishment thereof*' was circulated in the streets of London. The Privy Council rounded up as many copies as they could but Elizabeth was incandescent at this public criticism of a foreign prince, a guest in her realm and her potential husband. The author, a Puritan by the name of John Stubbs, was sentenced to lose his hand. The expected reprieve was not forthcoming, and the brutal punishment was carried out.

Elizabeth however, was not blind or deaf to the dissension within her Council, and, although negotiations carried on until 1581, this domestic uncertainty, together with her innate reluctance to marry, led her to call the negotiations to a halt on. In order to keep some of the advantages of the match, she lent Anjou money for campaigning in the Low Countries.

Once the match with Anjou had been broken off, it was clear to everyone that Elizabeth would never marry.

Chapter 11: Religious Dissent

Following the Act of Uniformity in 1559, Elizabeth was content that religious reform had gone far enough, but not everyone, including probably Cecil, agreed. Increasing in volume, were the radical Protestants, who became known as Puritans because of their objections to wearing the vestments laid down by the Act, and who strove throughout Elizabeth's reign to take reform further.

It can be inferred that Cecil was a supporter of a more radical settlement than Elizabeth eventually allowed. He favoured clerical marriage, which she did not; he pointedly refused to support Archbishop Parker's attempts to enforce conformity in the wearing of vestments, and he also supported the later Archbishop, Edmund Grindal in the dispute over 'prophesyings' with Elizabeth that ended in Grindal being relieved of his duties. But for Cecil, the enemies were the Catholics.

In 1558 Catholics were far and away the most populous group in the country, but, like most people in most times, the majority were not interested in religious martyrdom, and whatever their private thoughts, and sometimes practices, they attended church. Over the course of Elizabeth's reign, as new generations were brought up under the Act, the bulk of the population became Anglicans – essentially Protestant in doctrine, but dressed in the pared down Catholic clothes of ceremony.

A hard core of Catholics remained, and, as time went on, became more troublesome as religion and politics began to mix. In 1568, when Mary, Queen of Scots was deposed and fled to England, the Catholic party wished her to be openly recognised as Elizabeth's successor, and some even believed that she should already be Queen. For Cecil, this was an intolerable situation – he genuinely believed that the succession of Mary would lead to the re-imposition of Catholicism, and he feared that Elizabeth would be assassinated in order to bring the day forward.

Cecil heartily concurred with the advice of his close colleague, Sir Francis Walsingham that 'it is better to fear too much, than too little'. He saw plots everywhere, and his whole energies were directed to circumventing them, by fair means, and sometimes by foul.

Cecil's obsession with Catholic rebels at home, and his desire to support Protestant rebels abroad, had contributed to deteriorating relationships with Spain. The impounding, on Cecil's advice, of three Spanish ships carrying gold to the Low Countries for their armies that had taken refuge in Plymouth Sound, caused a serious rupture in diplomatic relationships. Many of Elizabeth's other Councillors, who were becoming restive under Cecil's dominance, felt he was provoking Spain too far.

A plan was hatched for Mary, Queen of Scots to marry Thomas Howard, 4th Duke of Norfolk, and a Protestant. Norfolk and Cecil were on bad terms. The proposal was supported not only by Norfolk's brother-in-law, the Earl of Westmorland, but also by the Protestant Earls of Leicester and Pembroke, and the Catholic Earl of Arundel. The Catholic Earl of Northumberland was not convinced of the merits of the plan, as he did not want Mary to marry a Protestant.

Elizabeth rejected the idea out of hand, and rebuked those Councillors who were criticising Cecil's handling of foreign policy. But negotiations continued in secret. In July, on a day when Cecil was absent from the

Privy Council, the majority agreed that if Mary married a Protestant, she could be freed. Still no-one dared to tell the Queen, until, on 6th September 1569, Leicester confessed all.

Norfolk withdrew from court, then, when he refused to answer Elizabeth's summons to Windsor, it was assumed that he had gone to his East Anglian estates to raise an army. In fact, he hadn't, and on 1st October wrote to Westmorland to desist from insurrection, whilst he returned to London to throw himself on Elizabeth's mercy.

The northern Earls, Northumberland and Westmorland decided to act anyway, although their activities were disorganised and somewhat half-hearted. Cecil's worst fears were recognised when they raised an army and marched to Durham Cathedral, where a full Roman Catholic Mass was offered. But, as with the Pilgrimage of Grace, thirty years earlier, the south was controlled by the government, and there was little support for the rising beyond the northern counties. By November, Cecil was reporting that:

'Our northern rebellion is fallen flat to the ground and scattered away.'

Cecil emerged from the affair stronger than ever, and his anti-Catholic stance seemed vindicated. Unpleasant rumours that he and Bacon were conspiring to have Norfolk (imprisoned in the Tower) murdered, were brushed off.

In 1570, the stakes were raised when the Pope finally excommunicated Elizabeth. In his Bull, *Regnans in Excelsis*, he not only pronounced the Queen a heretic, but also absolved all of her subjects of any oaths of allegiance they might have sworn to her. Even more provocatively, the Bull stated that any who obeyed the Queen would be cursed. The words *'I told you so,'* must have been trembling on Cecil's lips when Elizabeth heard that this was the result of her toleration of private Catholic practices, and her reluctance to deal too harshly with the Queen of Scots.

The Bull backfired spectacularly. The majority of law-abiding Catholic subjects had absolutely no intention of defying the Queen, or attempting to overthrow her. Even Philip of Spain thought the Bull was the wrong approach. For Cecil, it was grist to his mill. Parliament was called and new laws introduced to not only make it high treason for anyone to 'reconcile' to Rome, but also, it became treason to have any 'vain and superstitious things' such as crosses, relics, Agnus Dei etc, that had been blessed by the Pope or a priest.

The Commons removed the exemption from the Act of Uniformity, which had allowed gentlemen with private chapels to attend service there, rather than in the Parish Church, according to the authorised rite. They also tried to impose a requirement to take Communion, which would immediately identify every Catholic who refused. This latter clause was hotly debated. It was one thing to impose attendance, it was quite another to force someone to receive Communion.

The Lords (where Cecil was now seated as Lord Burghley) were not unanimous. At least four of them (Lords Vaux and Windsor and the Earls of Worcester and Southampton) voted against it. The Queen then vetoed the bill. She still would not force consciences (at least, not those of noblemen), provided outward conformity was observed. The cost of failure to attend church however, was increased, from 1s to £20, enough to ruin most families if they persisted in recusancy.

During the late 1570s, a new Catholic threat became apparent as the English seminary, established in Rome by the Englishman William Allen, and later taken over by the Jesuits, began to send priests into England on a mission both to reinvigorate the recusants, and convert people to the Roman Catholic faith. Within the movement there were many who wanted to concentrate only on religion, and not to embroil themselves in politics. In support of this, the Bull, *Regnans in Excelsis* was modified by Pope Gregory XIII who permitted English Catholics to obey the Queen in civil matters.

One of the most famous of these missionaries was Edmund Campion, who entered England in 1580, and was captured in 1581, tortured, condemned for treason, and hanged, drawn and quartered. There was much unease at the idea of persecution for religion. In 1583, Cecil wrote a tract, the *Execution of Justice*, defending the deaths of Campion and others and the allegations of torture. In it, he wrote that the torture of Campion had not, contrary to rumour, been so great that he could not walk. He also added that the rack had been managed

'*ever by those that attended upon the Examinations charged to use it (the rack) in as charitable Maner as such thing might be.*'

None of the men questioned had been asked about their religion, only about political matters, and whether, if the Pope commanded them to rebel, they would do so.

As for Alexander Bryant, from whom food and water had been withheld until he was obliged to lick the stones of his prison, well, it was his own fault. In an effort to gain a sample of his handwriting, he had been told to write something, anything, and had refused. He was then told he could have food and water if he would write his request down. His refusal to request food could hardly make the authorities guilty of starving him.

In Cecil's eyes, the hounding of Catholic priests was completely justified – they sought to overthrow the Protestant state, and kill the Queen. It was apparent that Spain was planning invasion, and the Queen of Scots was still attracting plots. Every weapon had to be used to protect England.

He wrote further advice to the Queen on how to manage Catholics who were suspected of supporting invasion. They should not, he advised, be asked to swear an oath that they would fight against any Popish invasion plans. To ask that would be to render them *'desperate'*, and his view was that desperate men would do desperate deeds. Besides the only way to get rid of desperate men is to kill them, and *'there are so many it would be as hard and difficult as it would be impious and ungodly'*.

Instead, the suspects should be asked to swear that anyone who refused to fight invasion plans ought to be condemned as a traitor. He believed that most would take the oath, as they were not being asked to comment on what they would do in the circumstances. Refusal to take it would immediately show the person as a traitor, but would not be a religious question.

In 1586, yet another plot against the Queen was discovered. It is certainly possible that the Babington Plot was a sting, manufactured by Cecil and Walsingham, but the Queen of Scots fell into the trap. Cecil was determined that this would be her end, and, when she was condemned in a trial at Fotheringhay Castle, over which Cecil presided, he pleaded with Elizabeth to sign the death warrant.

Elizabeth hesitated for weeks, but eventually signed it. Immediately the signed document was given to the Privy Council, which, before the Queen could change her mind, was sent to Fotheringhay and carried out. When she discovered what had happened, the Queen's rage, real or feigned, knew no bounds. She banished Cecil from court and refused to see him for months.

Still the Catholics refused to go away, and for the remainder of Elizabeth's reign the spectre of a Catholic invasion, supported by internal traitors, remained. Nevertheless, after the defeat of the Armada in 1588, it became obvious that there was no widespread support for foreign invasion or a forcible return to Rome. Although the penalties for recusancy were ruinous, and the government continued to vigorously seek out priests, dragging them from their priest holes, and fining and imprisoning those who harboured them, the level of fear somewhat subsided.

Chapter 12: Foreign Policy

Negotiations for Elizabeth's marriage were, of course, just one strand in England's foreign policy. Cecil's long-term goal of creating a single, Protestant, British state, and helping co-religionists across Europe was manifested in other ways, not always successfully, as Queen and minister did not necessarily agree on either aims or the right method to achieve them. Cecil was always a proponent of supporting of supporting Protestants abroad, although, conceptually, this had little appeal for Elizabeth who did not wish to give succour to people in rebellion against lawful authority.

England also needed to steer a course between the two European giants, France and Spain. Spain, and its associated territories, the Netherlands, had, historically, been England's ally. In particular, the Netherlands was the greatest market for English exports. Difficulties arose when the Netherlands wanted to throw off the dominion of its Spanish king, Philip II. Philip, from having been friendly disposed towards England, whose king he had once been, decided that it was his role in life to re-impose the Roman Catholic religion both in the Netherlands and England.

Queen and minister were at odds on what should be done. Cecil was eager to support the Netherlands, because a proportion (although not all) were Protestant. Elizabeth baulked at undermining royal authority. The other stumbling block was the activities of the French – they, too, were involving themselves, with a view to taking over the Netherlands. From Elizabeth's perspective, the possibility of French control was worse than Spanish.

In March 1572, England closed its borders to Dutch 'Sea-Beggars' who had been capturing Spanish shipping in the Channel. This brought about a rapprochement with Spain – relations having been frosty since the unravelling of the Ridolfi Plot, although by June, Philip was complaining that English interference was undermining his authority and Burghley (Cecil had been promoted to Baron Burghley that year) was informed that

'[King Philip] has sworn that he will be revenged in such sort, as both the Queen and England shall repent that ever they did meddle in any of his countries.'

On 24th August 1572, something occurred that reinforced Burghley's view of the urgent need for England to support co-religionists abroad. On that day, one of the worst massacres in Western European history since the fall of Rome began, carried out by the Catholics of France, against their Huguenot (French Protestant) countrymen. As many as 30,000 were killed in the days and weeks that followed.

At some point in 1572 (the memorandum is not accurately dated) Burghley set out the pros and cons of aiding the Dutch. We may infer, from the first article, that he did not share the note with the Queen.

'Objections – First, for that her Majesty being by sex fearful, cannot but be irresolute.

Secondly, in respect her Majesty is not furnished with such store of treasure as were requisite for a prince that is to enter into wars (money being the sinews of the same).

Thirdly, she is unfurnished of expert soldiers fit for the wars.

And again, (1) the wars may seem unjust and to maintain rebels

(2) In respect of the ancient league between [England] and [Spain];

(3) The greatness of the Prince with whom she is to contend [Philip]

(4) For that another [France] may grow over great.[1]

In favour of involvement, Burghley listed the fact that Spain had supported the Rising of the Northern Earls, that Philip's previous Governor in the Netherland, the Duke of Alba had slandered Elizabeth, that Spain was behind the Papal Bull excommunicating Elizabeth, and, most of all, that Philip was supporting Mary, Queen of Scots, and had sent a ship full of bullion to her party in Scotland (at that time torn between the Queen's Party and the King's Party). Positives to be gained were that:

By joining the enterprise her Majesty shall advance the cause of the religion; (2) her Majesty with her confederates shall give liberty to all Europe[2]

And further, that her intervention would take the glory away from the French Guise party that was supporting the Dutch – even though at home the Guises were militantly Catholic and violently supressing the Huguenots.

Although accused of interference, Elizabeth forbore to send troops to the Dutch leader, William of Orange in December of that year.

Elizabeth then made strenuous efforts to broker a peace when Philip's new deputy in the Netherlands, Don Luis de Requesens y Zúñiga, took a more conciliatory line with the rebels. The Spanish agreed to remove their troops, provided Catholicism was imposed and maintained. Elizabeth thought the Dutch should accept this compromise, and was

---

[1] http://www.british-history.ac.uk/cal-cecil-papers/vol2/pp29-42 Words in [] added.
[2] ibid.

displeased that William of Orange refused to do so. His desire for religious tolerance, was, she thought, quite indefensible and in 1575, Burghley was commanded to write to all the ports forbidding the landing of William of Orange or any of his supporters.

After Requesens' death in March 1576, and before the arrival of the new Governor, Philip's half-brother, Don Juan of Austria, the unpaid Spanish army sacked Antwerp, uniting the disparate rebel forces against Spain. Don John, whose ultimate mission appears to have been an invasion of England, followed by marriage to Mary, Queen of Scots and the taking of the English throne, was forced to comprise with the Dutch.

The Pacification of Ghent was agreed amongst Netherlandish states, agreeing to raise an army to resist Don Juan and Spain. Don Juan accepted terms, in the Perpetual Edict, agreeing that Spanish troops would return home. He planned to send them via England. Elizabeth immediately refused to allow them safe passage, believing it was but the cover for an invasion. Don Juan then broke the terms of the Perpetual Edict by capturing the town of Naumur.

Finally driven to involvement, Elizabeth authorised the sending of a large amount of cash to the Dutch. She was obliged to pawn her own jewels to raise it. She would not, however, openly intervene, instead, she carried on the discussions about a marriage to François, Duke of Alençon (later Duke of Anjou) with a view to controlling French activities in the Netherlands.

Over the following ten years, tensions escalated. More plots were uncovered to put Mary Queen of Scots on the throne; France was scarred by ugly and repeated religious civil wars, and the Dutch and Spanish continued to fight. In the early 1580s, Elizabeth was persuaded to direct intervention, although she and Burghley had qualms about the cost, and the risk of provoking Spain to the point of no return. The Earl of

Leicester was sent to represent England, and to lead her forces. Nothing was fully resolved, and, in the end, Leicester was withdrawn in 1587.

With the execution of Mary, Queen of Scots in 1587 which, for Burghley, was the triumphant vindication of his long campaign against her, there was no possibility of averting war with Spain. In another of his detailed memoranda, Burghley set out the best way to organise the Queen's troops and navy to forestall invasion.

He calculated the number of ships available to be 37, with 6,000 men, plus some further merchant shipping. He also hoped that some additional ships might be obtained from the King of Scots, since he might reasonably expect to succeed Elizabeth. The ships were to be divided into two fleets, one part to protect the entry to the channel from the west, and the other part at the eastern end. In all, he calculated that the costs of the ships, together with paying the men, victualling the ships, and providing arms would amount to some £60-70,000. In addition, an army would need to be raised and paid – at least £24,000 for two months. Then there was the necessity for men for the Scots border, for Ireland and for Kent, costing at least a further £20,000. He calculated that the costs the Queen had already incurred in the Netherlands were at least £130,000 per annum.

With these costs, and a treasury that was not overfull (inflation was a scourge in the sixteenth century), it was not surprising he also weighed up the advantages of making a treaty with Spain, even at that late point. For Burghley, though, no peace could be entered into unless Spain were willing to cede religious toleration to the Protestants in the Netherlands – he does not seem to have reflected that a similar religious toleration might be granted at home to Catholics.

With the defeat of the Armada of 1588, the worst threat to English security was past, although Spain made several further attempts to invade. With the accession in France of Henri of Navarre, a Huguenot who converted to Catholicism saying *'Paris is worth a Mass'*, there seemed less to fear from France as well.

Chapter 13: The Last Years

The last years of Burghley's life were by no means quiet, but after 1588, both he and Elizabeth seemed to enter a new phase. On the personal front, he suffered the loss of his mother, his wife and his daughter within the space of a year. His old colleagues and friends, the Earl of Leicester, Sir Francis Walsingham and Sir Christopher Hatton, died in the period 1588 – 1591 and their places at the Council table were being taken by a new generation.

Chief amongst these was Robert Devereux, Earl of Essex, who had been Burghley's ward. It was soon apparent that Essex was going to follow a very different path in the advice he gave the Queen than Burghley had. Essex loved the glory of war – he saw Burghley's cautious approach as pusillanimous at best, and perhaps even cowardly. He believed that England should carry the war against Spain into the enemy camp.

Whilst Essex retained his personal respect for Burghley, he did not extend such courtesy to Burghley's son, Robert Cecil, who was now also a member of the Privy Council. Robert and Essex were so temperamentally different that it was hard for them to work together, and their constant jarring created factions at court that Elizabeth was no longer able to control. The Essex faction criticised Robert Cecil, and by extension, Burghley's rule – accusing them of financial irregularity and corruption.

Burghley himself was in declining health. He had complained regularly over the years of gout, of being over burdened with work, and of needing rest. Indeed, one might believe him to be of a somewhat hypochondriacal turn of mind to read all of his complaints about headaches, stomach-aches, sore eyes and trembling hands. A constant refrain was '*I have been and yet am, not in sure health.*'

But by the 1590s, with Burghley well into his seventies, we might perhaps believe that he was indeed ill. He began to spend months away from the court. In April 1591, he attempted to retire, but Elizabeth, not seeing any diminution in his abilities refused. In a letter to him she called him by the pet name of Sir Spirit – it was her custom to give her favourites nicknames – and teased him about becoming the '*hermit of Theobalds.*'

His work carried on. Trouble in Ireland was mounting, and there was no easy solution as Spain funded the rebellion of the Irish Earls. The English had never had a complete domination of Ireland, and the Reformation had not penetrated much beyond the handful of Anglo-Irish in Dublin. Much of Burghley's advice was now given to Elizabeth via the mouth of Robert, as he spent increasing time confined to home with illness.

Vast amounts of correspondence on subjects as disparate as the funeral arrangements to be made for Henry Hastings, Earl of Huntingdon, Lord President of the Council of the North, and the state affairs at the court of the Duke of Brunswick were still delivered to him personally.

In 1597, he began to settle his affairs. He drew up regulations for an almshouse for thirteen poor men of Stamford, to be located near to the site of the school he had attended seventy years before. Although he had eschewed the mediaeval idea of prayers for the dead, yet, in his rules about the requirements for the inmates to wear his livery and attend church each Sunday, on pain of a fine, perhaps there was a trace of the old belief that the prayers of the living could help him, once dead.

He wrote his Will, carefully dividing his lands between his elder son, Thomas, who was to have Burghley and the family estates around Stamford, and Robert, who was to have Theobalds.

In April 1598, he was given leave to absent himself from the annual Garter ceremony. He then travelled to Theobalds for a few weeks in June before returning to London and attending council meetings.

Finally, he took to his bed at Cecil House, where Elizabeth came in person to see him and fed him with her own hands. By 21st July he had an infected throat, perhaps a quinsy, and he died on the morning of 4th August, 1598. One of his last known letters was to his son, Robert, in which he summed up his life of service:

'Serve God by serving the Queen, for all other service is indeed bondage to the Devil.'

Aspects of the life of Sir William Cecil, Lord Burghley

Chapter 14: Key Dates in his life

1520	Born, 14th September, Bourne, Lincolnshire
c. 1528	To school at Grantham
c. 1530	To school at Stamford
May 1535	To St John's College, Cambridge
1540	Began studying at Gray's Inn, London
6 May 1541	Admitted, Gray's Inn
August 1541	Married Mary Cheke of Cambridge, sister of John Cheke
May 1542	Birth of son, Thomas, later Earl of Exeter
22 February 1544	Death of Mary
24 December 1545	Married Mildred Cooke, daughter of Sir Anthony Cooke
1543 – 44	May have sat in the House of Commons. This Parliament passed the 3rd Succession Act
c. 1545	Enters the service of Edward Seymour, Earl of Hertford
1545	Recorder of Boston

28 January 1547	Death of Henry VIII
February 1547	Earl of Hertford becomes Lord Protector and Duke of Somerset
1547	Justice of the Peace, Lincolnshire
1548	Master of Requests for Duke of Somerset
1549	Buys lease of the Rectory, Wimbledon
1549	First Book of Common Prayer
6 July 1549	Custos Rotulorum for Lincolnshire
10 September 1549	Present at Battle of Pinkie
24 November 1549	Arrested and imprisoned in the Tower of London
25 January 1550	Released from the Tower
5 September 1550	Secretary to Edward VI and appointed to Privy Council
c. 1550	Steward to the Lady Elizabeth of her lands in Lincolnshire
11th October 1551	Knighted
Before 1552	Court of Augmentations for Lincolnshire
22nd January 1552	Execution of Edward Seymour, Duke of Somerset
1552	Second Book of Common Prayer
19 March 1553	Death of his father, Richard Cecil

12 April 1553	Chancellor of the Order of the Garter
6 July 1553	Death of Edward VI
8 August 1553	Took part in funeral of Edward VI at Westminster Abbey
22 August 1553	Execution of John Dudley, Duke of Northumberland
1554	Birth and death of Frances Cecil
1554	Travelled to Brussels to meet Cardinal Pole and escort him home
1555	Member of the House of Commons
1556	Steward of the Manor of Wimbledon for Cardinal Pole
5 Dec 1556	Birth of Anne 'Nan' Cecil, later Countess of Oxford
17 November 1558	Death of Mary I and accession of Elizabeth I
20 November 1558	Sworn in as Privy Councillor and Secretary
1559	Birth and death of William Cecil (I)
1559	Act of Uniformity
c. 1560	Steward of Stamford, Lincolnshire
1560	Acquired Theobalds
1560	Visited Scotland to negotiate Treaty of Edinburgh
1561	Birth and death of William Cecil (II)

1563	Birth of Robert Cecil, later Earl of Salisbury
1563	Elected senior Knight of the Shire for Northamptonshire and Lincolnshire
1563	High Steward of Westminster
1564	Birth of Elizabeth Cecil, later Lady Wentworth
10 January 1568	Master of the Court of Wards and Liveries
1568	Lord Lieutenant of Middlesex
1569	Rising of the Northern Earls
April – June 1571	Lord Keeper of the Privy Seal
7 September 1571	Execution of Thomas Howard, 4th Duke of Norfolk
25 February 1572	Created 1st Baron of Burghley
July 1572	Lord Treasurer
4 August 1572	The Massacre of St Bartholomew
1572	Overseer of the Queen's Majesty's Works
April 1583	Death of Elizabeth Cecil, Lady Wentworth
1585	Steward of the Honour of Bolingbroke, Lincolnshire
1587	Lord Lieutenant of Lincolnshire
8 February 1587	Execution of Mary, Queen of Scots

1588	Lord Lieutenant of Essex and Hertfordshire
10 March 1588	Death of Jane Heckingon, Mrs Cecil, his mother
5 June 1588	Death of Anne Cecil, Countess of Oxford
7 August 1588	Defeat of Spanish Armada
4 April 1589	Death of Mildred Cooke, Lady Burghley, his wife
15 July 1598	Last attendance at a Council meeting
4 August 1598	Death of Sir William Cecil, Lord Burghley

Chapter 15: Family Life

Marriage

William Cecil first married in around August 1541. His bride was Mary Cheke, sister of his friend and tutor at Cambridge, John Cheke. Almost nothing is known of Mary, other than that her father had died before 1541, and that she lived in the house of her mother, Agnes, who was a vintner and small business-woman, established near St John's College. As well as John, Mary had four other siblings, Elizabeth, Alice, Magdalen and Anne, who lived to adulthood. We can infer that Cecil was on good terms with the whole family, as Anne Cheke's son, Hugh Alington, later became one of his secretaries.

At the time of Cecil's marriage to Mary, her brother had not yet achieved the prestige he attained later as Regius Professor of Greek, and tutor to Prince Edward, and so, from the point of view of Cecil's father, the match was a disappointment. The purpose of matrimony was to extend a family's influence, not the indulgence of private affection. Soon after his marriage, Cecil was sent to Gray's Inn to continue his studies, but was obliged to leave Mary behind. Presumably, still financially dependent on his father, he could not afford to maintain her in London.

In May, 1542, Mary gave birth to a son, Thomas. In February of the following year, she died, although the cause is unknown, as is the frequency with which she and Cecil met during the years of their marriage. Based in London, he would have had little spare cash for visiting her. After her death, Thomas remained in Cambridge with his grandmother, Agnes Cheke. Agnes paid Mary's funeral expenses of 6s 8d.

There is no record of Cecil's reaction to Mary's death, but, since he continued to be close friends with John Cheke, we can suppose that they shared their grief.

Cecil's second marriage was far more to the taste of his family. The lady was Mildred Cooke, one of the seven (or possibly eight) children of Anthony Cooke, who, like Cecil's father, was a member of Henry VIII's household. Mildred is usually listed on genealogical sites as the eldest daughter, but, given the naming practices of the time, it is more likely that Anne was the eldest, named for her mother and grandmother. Mildred was named for her step-grandmother.

Cooke was a member of the royal bodyguard, but there was certainly more to him than brawn. Like his new son-in-law, he was trained for the law, although, in Cooke's case, his Inn was Inner Temple. Cooke was a dedicated promoter of education, and his five daughters received the same education as his sons, in Latin and Greek. Two of them, Anne and Mildred, became noted scholars, whilst a third, Elizabeth was known as a poet and accomplished musician. Anthony Cooke was later involved in the tuition of Edward VI, although he was not formally the Prince's tutor.

Mildred was described (in bad verse!) as:

'Cooke is comely and thereto
In books sets all her care
In learning with the Roman dames
Of right she may compare.'

On this second marriage, which took place on 24th December 1545, Richard Cecil granted William and his bride land in Rutland and Leicestershire. Presumably Mildred also brought a dowry in either cash or land. This enabled them to set up a household, although there was no thought of leaving London.

Cooke was a member of the Reforming faction at Henry VIII's court, and all of his children followed him in this regard – two of his daughters later being known for their Puritan views. Cecil would have felt quite at home in these circles.

There is no information as to exactly where Cecil and Mildred lived immediately after their marriage – most likely, they had lodgings near Gray's Inn. In 1549, once Cecil was a member of the household of the Duke of Somerset, they took up residence at the Rectory, Wimbledon, although they also had a town house in Cannon Row, Westminster. Sharing their home at Wimbledon were Cecil's sister Mary, and Mildred's sister Elizabeth, as well as two wards – Arthur Hall and John Stanhope.

Whilst Cecil was serving Somerset, Mildred was developing her relationship with his wife, Anne Stanhope. She translated a sermon by St Basil the Great on the biblical book, *Deuteronomy*, that she dedicated to the Duchess, and signed, herself, in the usual deferential sixteenth century fashion as the Duchess' '*humble servant and debtor*'.

During these first years of married life, there were family visits to pay: to Burghley to see the senior Cecils, with side visits to Katherine, Dowager Duchess of Suffolk at Grimesthorpe, and Lord Clinton (once married to Bessie Blount): to Ingatestone Hall to visit Cecil's colleague, Sir William Petre; and, later, to Bisham to visit Mildred's sister, Elizabeth, who married Sir Thomas Hoby.

A Growing Family

One of Mildred's attractions as a match for Cecil had been her connections, and the promise of this seemed to be fulfilled when her brother married the cousin of Lady Jane Grey, a young woman who, in the early 1550s was talked of as a possible wife for Edward VI. In the event, Lady Jane was proclaimed Queen herself, with disastrous results. Whilst the plan for Jane to take the throne was being hatched, Cecil was covering his back with carefully placed statements to his friends and family, suggesting reluctance to be involved. He even wrote to Mildred, asking her, in the event of his death in the commotion likely to follow an attempt to subvert the succession, to continue to look after his son, Thomas. Should she decide to marry again, she should chose a man of good (ie Protestant) religion.

No children other than Thomas were mentioned, because, although Mildred's mother had had at least seven children in fairly quick succession, she and Cecil seem to have had some difficulty in beginning a family, and during Edward VI's reign, so far as is known, they had no children.

Thomas seems to have moved to live with William and Mildred when they took the house in Wimbledon. However, it appears that family life was difficult. Cecil did not get on well with his son, either when he was a child, or later. He admitted in May 1561 that

'To this hour I never showed any fatherly favour to him but in teaching and correcting.'

The result was, that, although there was never any open breach, there was little warmth between them. There is a record of them practising archery together in 1556, when Thomas was about eighteen. Hopefully, it was an enjoyable event, although one can image Cecil may have spent much of the afternoon carping at Thomas' style.

On Mary's accession, Mildred's sister, Anne, who was married to the Master of the Court of Wards, Sir Nicholas Bacon, became a part of the new Queen's household. Later, a third sister, Margaret Cooke, also served Queen Mary. This link to the Queen's household helped to maintain the Cecils' profile during Mary's reign, and both Cecil and Mildred visited Cardinal Pole and attended some of his sermons.

In 1554, Mildred gave birth to her first known child, a daughter, named Frances, presumably for Frances, Duchess of Suffolk, who, despite the execution of her husband and daughter, Lady Jane Grey, remained in favour with Queen Mary. Cecil later wrote of the arrival in his commonplace book:

> *'Between 11 and 12 this night my wife gave birth to a daughter called Frances but after a few hours the tiny girl departed this mortal life and was buried at Wimbledon.'*

In 1555, Cecil paid the dowry of his sister, Elizabeth, on her marriage to Robert Wingfield. He did not forget his father-in-law, who had chosen to leave England on Mary's succession, for the more attractive, Protestant air of Strasbourg. Cecil sent him money regularly, and, no doubt thinking of him as well as his other Protestant friends, voted against a government bill that year to deprive exiles of their lands.

The Cecils were invited in July of 1556 to visit their friend, Sir Philip Hoby, at his home at Bisham. Sir Philip even offered to send a carriage for Mildred, as she was expecting. Probably fearing the jolting of the unsprung carriages of the time, the Cecils declined. Their carefulness paid off, as, on 5th December, a healthy daughter was born, named Anne, presumably for Mildred's mother and sister, or perhaps for her godmother Anne, Lady Petre. The Petres also gave a sumptuous gift of a gilt salt cellar.

Sir Philip Hoby also sent his congratulations, lamenting slightly that Anne was not that far more worthy creature, a son:

> *'Of my lady's daughter (in hope of a son hereafter), I trust ye be now no sorrowful man.'*

Congratulations were also received from Cecil's father-in-law, no doubt now relieved that his daughter was finally showing signs of knowing her duty. He hoped that Mildred would *'increase [Cecil] with many sons and daughters, though she were not hasty at the beginning.'*

These words tend to dispel any thoughts that Mildred had suffered many miscarriages or infant deaths previously.

Cecil adored his little girl, referred to as Nan, or even Tannikin, in family correspondence. When she was nine, he even wrote a poem for her – rather different from his usual dry outpourings. It went with her New Year gift of a toy spinning wheel. Ever the improving father, the gift was to encourage her *some thrift to feel* in learning a housewife's tasks.

William and Mildred had two more children who lived to adulthood. Robert, born 1 June 1563, and Elizabeth, born 1 July 1564. There were two short-lived boys, both named William, who were born in 1559 and 1561. Robert too, although he survived, was not especially robust – he had some physical deformity which gave him a curvature of the spine.

Thomas

In 1561, Cecil's oldest child, Thomas, was ready to embark on adult life. He had been well educated by Cambridge tutors (although there is no record of him attending the university – his masters came to him). He had also been taught the appropriate courtly arts of dancing and music. Thus armed, Cecil sent him to Paris to practice his French and learn to be a courtier.

Thomas was to be accompanied by one of his father's clerks, Thomas Windebank, who was furnished with £90 in gold for the trip. Obviously, Cecil didn't believe his son was sufficiently mature to hold the cash himself. The original plan was for Thomas to spend time both at the French court, where Cecil's friend, Sir Nicholas Throckmorton, was Ambassador, and also to meet other Englishmen – chief of whom was the Earl of Hertford who had been sent abroad earlier that year. When the scandal of Hertford's secret marriage to the Queen's cousin, Lady Katherine Grey, came to light, Cecil was quick to send a message to Thomas to avoid Hertford's company.

Unsurprisingly, given his first taste of freedom, Thomas did not always behave in ways his father approved of. There was the usual problem of the expenses of a young man outstripping his allowance. In particular, Thomas' purchase of a horse drew disapproving letters from his father. A man of Thomas' age and station in life should be content to walk. Cecil summed up his fears by writing to Windebank that he feared Thomas would return *'like a spending sot [drunkard], meet to keep a tennis court.'* Why tennis-court-keeping or using should be disgraceful is a mystery, but clearly it upset Cecil. He continued to send reprimands and harsh messages about his disappointment in his son's behaviour to Thomas until the young man returned.

Whether Thomas were the ideal son in terms of his behaviour or not, he quickly proved that he could fulfil the obligation on every gentleman to marry well. In 1564, he married Dorothy Neville, the daughter of John Neville, 4th Baron Latimer, who had once been step-son to Queen Katherine Parr. Whilst his father had a small family by the standards of the day, Thomas and Dorothy produced thirteen children. His descendants continue to hold the Marquessate of Exeter.

Thomas played little part in public life. He was an officer in the army sent by the government to repress the Rising of the Northern Earls in 1569, and, bizarrely, together with his half-brother, Robert, was intended to be the target of a kidnapping plot a couple of years later. The conspirators, whose primary plan had been to assassinate William Cecil (by then Lord Burghley) as part of their overall scheme to enthrone Mary, Queen of Scots, had planned to capture the Cecil brothers to ransom them should the murder of Cecil go awry. Nothing came of this, or any other of the various assassination plots of Elizabeth's reign.

A request by Thomas in 1575 for a passport to travel abroad was refused by the Queen, and we can infer that Cecil had asked her to reject it, as he did not want Thomas to travel whilst the latter's eldest son, another William, was underage.

As time passed, Thomas and his father seem to have been on better terms. In 1575, Thomas wrote, requesting Cecil to ensure that Mildred and Anne should visit Wimbledon. It would, he said, presumably without sarcasm, be '*a comfort unto my wife and me, and an honour to my poor parsonage.*'

Anne and Elizabeth

Anne was the second of Cecil's children to marry. A betrothal had been arranged for her when she was twelve, in 1568. This was to Philip Sidney, son of Sir Henry Sidney, President of the Council of Wales, and his wife, Mary Dudley, daughter of Cecil's old master, the Duke of Northumberland. Although contracts were signed, the wedding was never carried out. Instead, Anne made what was, on paper, a far grander match – to a man well known to her before-hand – Edward de Vere, Earl of Oxford. Oxford was one of Cecil's wards, and had joined the household in 1564 when he was thirteen. Cecil, responsible for his upbringing and his estates, made careful arrangements for both.

The couple were married on 19 December 1571, in the presence of the Queen. The marriage turned out to be one of the most miserable of the era. In 1573, Oxford had licence to travel abroad. Whilst he was away, Anne gave birth to a daughter, whom she named Elizabeth. Oxford thanked Cecil for sending him the news and dispatched presents for Anne, but, when he returned home, he refused to acknowledge the child and sent Anne back to her parents, with bitter words. He had, apparently, some '*mislikings*' of Anne or her behaviour, but he refused to specify what. In an age when female chastity was considered her most important virtue, the disgrace that Anne suffered when rejected by her husband, and the hints that her daughter was not his, must have been hard for her to bear. Cecil and Mildred stood by her throughout, and for the next few years, she lived with them.

At some point in the early 1580s there was a partial reconciliation between the Oxfords. Anne produced a son, who died within a few hours, and then two more daughters, Bridget and Frances. Nevertheless, there were long periods when the Earl would refuse to have anything to do with his wife, and would leave her to live at her parents' expense. Anne died young, only 31, on 5 June 1587. She was buried in Westminster Abbey.

Cecil's other daughter, Elizabeth, did not make so grand a match as her sister. Aged 18 in 1582, she married the 26 year old William Wentworth, son of Lord Wentworth, an old friend of Cecil's. It appears from the correspondence, that the couple fell in love, and Wentworth requested his father to make overtures to Cecil. Perhaps chastened by the unhappiness of Anne, Cecil did not seek to make a second grand match, and Elizabeth and Wentworth were married in February 1582. But this marriage too, ended badly. The groom was dead by November, and Elizabeth followed him to the grave in April 1583.

Robert

Cecil's second son, Robert, was initially more successful in his marital career than his sisters. He married Elizabeth Brooke, the daughter of 10th Lord Cobham in 1586, when he was 22. The couple had three children before Elizabeth's untimely death in 1597. Robert mourned her deeply and, unusually, never remarried. His descendants are the Marquesses of Salisbury.

Robert was certainly more successful in his political career than his brother. It seems that Cecil groomed him from an early age to be his political heir. Perhaps Robert's physical infirmity made him more interested in studying and politics, or perhaps Cecil had learnt from the mistakes he made with Thomas and spent more time with his younger son. Robert received expert tuition in Latin, Greek, Mathematics and all of the other subjects considered essential to the Humanist education. He then went on to study law at Gray's Inn, where he was admitted in 1580. Following that, he travelled abroad for a short period.

Whatever the reason, Cecil made every attempt to promote Robert's career at court.

Like his brother, twenty years before, Robert travelled abroad for a short period, studying at the Sorbonne. When he came home, he sat in the House of Commons for Westminster. By 1587, Cecil was promoting him to the Queen as a suitable man to take over some over some of his duties, a message he repeated over the next few years. Eventually, in 1596, Elizabeth appointed Robert to the role of Secretary – the position Cecil had held when she first came to the throne. But such a promotion caused a good deal of envy at court – particularly in the faction surrounding the Earl of Essex, and his sister, Lady Penelope Rich.

The late 1580s were a time of loss for Cecil. In the period 1588, he lost his daughter Anne, his mother (who must have been getting on for ninety), and then, in 1589, his wife of over forty years. His grief was heavy. He wrote that they had

'lived in continual love without any separation or any offence.'

Mildred was buried with her daughter, Anne, Countess of Oxford in Westminster Abbey. Cecil paid for a sumptuous monument, in which the two of them are surrounded by the kneeling figures of Anne's daughters, Lady Elizabeth, Lady Bridget and Lady Susan de Vere, and Mildred's son, Robert.

Despite this, when his own time came, Cecil chose to be buried in Stamford, by the side of his parents, in the country he always thought of as his.

Chapter 16: Architect & Builder

In modern parlance, Cecil was a workaholic. He worked by day and night, writing the vast majority of his letters in his own hand, and working out arguments by creating long lists of pros and cons. But even the busiest man needs some outlet for his creative energies, and Cecil's artistic bent found its expression in architecture. Architecture was one of the most fashionable pursuits of gentlemen in the Renaissance period – it was used to express power and wealth as well as taste and education, and there is no doubt Cecil wanted to indicate that he possessed all of those attributes.

During his long life and political career, Cecil built three vast properties that typified the Elizabethan style. Sadly, only one remains - Burghley House. The other two, Cecil House on the Strand, London, and Theobalds (bizarrely, pronounced Tibbalds), near Cheshunt, in Hertfordshire, just north of London, have left no traces. Nevertheless, from the copious records kept, we can learn a bit about them. He also built or renovated two other houses – one named Pymmes at Edmonton (not far from Theobalds) and one at Chelsea, in London, although we cannot find any direct evidence of ownership or any reason for him to have a property there.

Architecture was a taste that Cecil first seems to have developed during Edward VI's reign. His patron, the Duke of Somerset, built the vast Somerset House in the Strand – the first great construction by a subject since Wolsey had created Hampton Court, some thirty years before. Whilst he was Somerset's Master of Requests, it is likely that Cecil visited frequently, and, it appears he was impressed by it, as the West Gate he built at Burghley resembled the earlier construction.

Other members of Somerset's household who were friends of Cecil's were Sir Thomas Smith and Sir John Thynne, builders of Hill Hall, Essex (now owned by English Heritage) and Longleat, in Wiltshire, respectively. Longleat, currently lived in by a descendant of Thynne, is similar in style to Burghley House, and we can speculate that Cecil and Thynne conferred.

The fall of Somerset did not put an end to architectural discussion at court – the Duke of Northumberland was also interested in the practice, and sent John Shute, author of the first English treatise on architecture, to Italy. Doubtless Cecil was fascinated by what Shute discovered there and would have read Shute's work - *The First and Chief Grounds of Architecture.*

As well as Somerset House and Longleat, another model for Burghley was Sir Thomas Gresham's new Exchange, in the City of London, the stone loggia (an open arcade) of which was originally copied at Burghley, although it was later covered in.

According to his early biographer, the Rev. W.B Charlton, who was chaplain to the Marquess of Exeter in the 1840s, Cecil's father, Richard, was granted the former priory of St Michael's, Stamford together with 299 acres of arable land in 1539. This became the nucleus of the modern Burghley estate, and Cecil began working on it after his father's death in 1553. It remained the principal house of his mother, Jane, until her death in 1588. The original works, carried out in the 1550s and 1560s, were later replaced with even grander edifices.

Cecil's great masterpiece was Theobalds. He acquired the land, just west off what is now the A10 some time around 1560. He probably chose the location as handy for travelling between Cecil House in the Strand, and Burghley. Information about one of his journeys between his previous house in Wimbledon and Burghley show that this is the route he customarily took.

Major works seem to have begun in the late 1560s – in 1572 alone, he spent £2,700. The property was finally finished in 1585. There are some 18 drawings still extant in the archives at Hatfield House (which Cecil's son, Sir Robert, acquired in exchange for Theobalds when James VI & I made clear his desire to own the great pleasure palace himself). From the annotations on the drawings, it can be inferred that Cecil himself was, at least in part, his own architect and designer. He appears to have been able to draw well – there is a note from a mason at building asking him to send a detailed drawing, so that he can understand what is required.

Once completed, the house was vast – the domestic parts of the building set around two large courtyards or quadrangles, and smaller ones for the buttery, the dial (clock) and the dovecotes. There was also a long gallery and a hall.

The main quadrangle, Fountain Court, was 86 ft square and housed a water feature of black and white marble. On the east of the court was an open loggia, floored with Purbeck marble, presumably for walking in to catch the evening sun.

The location made Theobalds a convenient place for Elizabeth I to travel to when she wished to leave London for a spot of hunting. She paid Burghley repeated visits over the years, the first being in 1564, when she apparently complained that her bedroom was too small, leading him, or so he claimed, to enlarge the house. It was still not complete by the time she arrived again on 22nd September 1571. Rather than the Queen bringing a gift with her for her hostess, she was the recipient of some verses (one's ears cringe at the thought) and a picture of the house.

Whether it was the house or the company she most enjoyed, she visited again in 1572, 1575, 1577, 1583, 1587, 1591, 1593, 1594 and 1596.

Sometimes her stay was of brief duration, but on other occasions she brought a large retinue with her. Elizabeth, perennially short of money, and of a thrifty turn of mind, was always happy for her courtiers to support some of the financial burden of the court. In 1583, she was accompanied by her friend, Robert, Earl of Leicester; his brother, the Earl of Warwick; her other favourite, Sir Christopher Hatton; Cecil's companion and colleague, Sir Francis Walsingham; the Queen's cousin, Lord Hunsdon, and several others.

Ten years later, she visited for nine days at a cost to Cecil (who was also of a frugal nature, and must have wilted under the bills) of nearly £3,000. With such sumptuous hospitality available, it was not unknown for Elizabeth to invite foreign ambassadors and dignitaries to wait upon her at Theobalds – the house and gardens were beautiful, and Cecil was picking up the tab!

To give this sum some context, his usual weekly bills at Theobalds were around £80 and his annual stabling bill was about £667. He paid £10 per week for the local unemployed to work in the gardens, and distributed £1 per week in charity. According to custom, even when Cecil was not in residence himself, there was provision for a table of gentleman and two tables of '*inferior*' persons for dinner each day. His silver plate weighed some 14,000 pounds (c. 6,350kg).

One of Cecil's favourite recreations was to ride around his gardens at Theobalds, on a mule.

Elizabeth would also visit Cecil at his town house, dining there on at least one occasion and attending the christening of his daughter, Elizabeth, to whom she stood as godmother. Cecil House, of which no trace now remains, was located on the Strand, north of where the Savoy Theatre now stands. It was built of brick, with four turrets and two courtyards. On the east range were the family's private apartments. To the north, the gardens stretched as far as what is now Covent Garden.

Cecil's interest in building presumably led to his appointment as Overseer of the Queen's Majesty's Works in 1572, although his job was probably to oversee the finances. The Comptroller of the Works, from 1556 – 1596, was one Thomas Fowler, with whom Cecil was on good terms, as may be inferred from the fact that Fowler bequeathed his house to Cecil, should he wish to accept it. Other men within the office were

Thomas Graves, Surveyor of the Queen's Works from 1578, Henry Hawthorn and John Symonds; drawings from the men remain in the archive at Hatfield. Graves seems to have worked for Cecil on the manor house at Pymmes, which Cecil purchased in 1582, paying £250 for six acres of pasture and a manor house. Once completed, it was lived in, after his marriage, by Cecil's younger son, Robert.

Chapter 17: Bibliophile & Map Collector

Sir William Cecil was educated at St John's College, Cambridge, one of the most advanced of the colleges at the time. His friends and colleagues there were all followers of the new humanist ideas that promoted the examination of original texts rather than the endless interpretations and reinterpretations of the works of the mediaeval scholars.

With the fall of Constantinople in 1453, the last remnants of the Roman Empire, a torrent of ancient manuscripts found its way into Europe, in Greek as well as Latin, which inspired the generations that followed to study Greek and classical Latin, rather than the mediaeval Latin into which it had metamorphosed. During his time in Cambridge, and after, Cecil was friends with some of the foremost scholars of the century – Roger Ascham, John Cheke, Thomas Smith. He himself, although never inclining to a career as an academic, never lost his interest in intellectual matters, even though his own writing style was somewhat turgid.

Throughout out his life, Cecil sought to learn, to gather facts and to know as much as he could about myriad topics, and this was reflected in a passion for collecting books and maps. Between January 1554 and December of the following year, a period during which his political career had taken a pause, there are seventy entries in his accounts for book purchases from the London book-seller William Seres. They include titles on cosmology, geography and navigation, reflecting his interests in maps and the physical world.

On his death in 1598, his will directed that his elder son, Thomas, should inherit '*all my books in my upper library over my Great chamber in my.... house in Westminster*' together with '*all my evidence and rolls belonging to my pedigrees*'. In common with most gentlemen of the era, Cecil liked to study genealogy and family trees, mainly in the hope of finding illustrious ancestors.

On a sale of some of the Cecil family's possessions in 1687, the inventory for books listed some 3,645 books and 249 volumes of manuscripts said to be his. The collection is now in four main parts – a great many are in the Cotton Collection at the British Museum, some are in the National Archive, a substantial portion is at Trinity College, Dublin, of which Cecil was Chancellor, and many remain at Hatfield House.

The collection includes mathematical, surveying, mapmaking, artillery building, town planning, and hydrography works.

One of the books in the collection is his Commonplace book (a kind of journal in which information was gathered, notes made and expenses recorded). Cecil's has a cover of vellum, folded to make a pocket, in which is stored a map of Sicily and one of the British Isles. It also has the distances and travel information for journeys between Antwerp and Dunkirk and Augsburg; and London to Edinburgh. Presumably the information dates from his trip to the continent during Mary's reign, and his expedition to Edinburgh to negotiate the eponymous treaty in 1560.

It appears that whilst Cecil liked maps, it was a cerebral matter, rather than a desire for travel, as, according to Henry Peacham's book, *The Compleat Gentleman*, published in 1622:

'If anyone came to the lords of the council for a licence to travel, he would first examine him of England; if he found him ignorant, would bid him stay at home and know his own country first.'

In 1563, Laurence Nowell, an early antiquarian and manuscript collector who worked for Cecil, wrote to him in for support for a map making project. Nowell, using the best butter, referred to Cecil's *'marvellous pleasure in geographical maps, above all other monuments of the noble arts.'* Cecil commissioned him to undertake a map of a part of the coast of Ireland, and it is likely that Nowell created Cecil's pocket map of the British Isles referred to above.

Cecil also collected maps from abroad. On 20 February 1567 he wrote to Sir Henry Norris, the English Ambassador to France, saying *'if there be any charts newly printed, I pray you send me a calendar thereof.'* Norris must have found some, as there is a letter from the following July, thanking him for the chart of Paris.

In around 1566, Cecil acquired a collection of engraved maps, compiled in Rome. It is likely that Nowell acted for him.

On 20 May 1570, Cecil acquired one of the earliest copies of *Theatrum Orbis Terrarum* the first modern atlas, published that year by the Flemish cartographer, Abraham Ortelius. Cecil hand-wrote his own notes on it.

He also kept detailed notes on the county atlases he collected. These were created during the period 1574 – 1578 by Christopher Saxon. They were engraved plates, and were delivered to Cecil as they were completed. On them, he annotated all the justices in England and Wales, added and corrected place names as well as supplementing the maps with historical, topographical and geographic notes and tables of roads and posts.

In addition to Saxon's maps, he collected a further 18 manuscript and two other printed maps of the British Isles, before 1595. These were remarked on by a foreign visitor to Theobalds, who noted hanging on the walls:

> 'correct landscapes of all the most important and remarkable towns in Christendom' and in another room, 'the Kingdom of England, with all its cities, towns and villages, mountains and rivers.'

His interest in maps was obviously widely known. He received presentation copies of the Dutch hydro-cartographer Lucas Waghenaer's work *De Spieghel Der Zeevaerdt*. This was translated into English on the orders of the Privy Council, by Anthony Ashley. Cecil took two copies, one to admire, and the other to use as a working copy.

He also had a plan of the Spanish palace, the Escorial, and maps of Guiana sent to him by Sir Walter Raleigh and Thomas Hariot.

Finally, Cecil's treasures included a *'lytle terrestriall Globe with a Lattin Booke that Teacheth the use of my great Globes'*. These great globes were made by Emery Molyneux and were 25 inches (c 60cm) in diameter.

Chapter 18: Following the Footsteps of William Cecil

Cecil was a Lincolnshire man, born and bred, and he always saw that county as his own. But as a politician, he needed to keep close to the centre of power and he spent the majority of his life in and around the capital, building several houses to reflect his status. He visited Scotland twice, once in peace, and once in war, and had two short trips abroad.

The numbers in the article below correspond to those on the map which follows.

*

When William Cecil was born in 1520 in the small town of Bourne (1) in Lincolnshire, it was to a family that, on his mother's side, was well-established in the district, with a history of service in the various civic offices of Bourne and membership of the religious guilds of the town. His father's family had settled in the neighbouring town of Stamford only in the last quarter of the fifteenth century, having come from South Wales, probably because of their connection, through the god-father of William's father Richard, with Lady Margaret Beaufort. Lady Margaret had an impressive estate nearby at Collyweston, and the Cecils had roles in its management. Thirty years later, William was to be steward of some of those lands on behalf of Lady Margaret's grand-daughter, Elizabeth.

William was christened in the Abbey Church of St Peter and St Paul, which, generally referred to as Bourne Abbey, still stands in the town, although the monastic buildings are long gone. At the time, the Abbey was an Augustinian foundation, at the heart of town life and Cecil's maternal grandparents are buried there.

Around 15 miles from Bourne is the large town of Grantham. Situated just off the A1, or in more romantic parlance, the Great North Road, it has been a settlement probably since Neolithic times. It was certainly in existence at the time of the Domesday Book in 1086. In the older part of the town is the enormous church of St Wulfram, noted in Simon Jenkins' '1000 Best Churches in England', as having the best steeple (282 ft in height) in the country. In the shadow of this enormous edifice is the old schoolhouse (2) that Cecil would have known when he came to be educated there. Cecil probably arrived not long after the school had been re-founded by Dr Richard Foxe, Bishop of Winchester, and once Lord Privy Seal.

Perhaps because of his youth, Cecil did not remain so far from home for long. Instead, he was moved to a school rather closer at Stamford (3). Stamford, like Grantham, is a settlement on the Great North Road. It is one of the loveliest towns in the whole of England, built of the local oolitic limestone, a hard-wearing, creamy stone. The town is home to an extraordinary number of mediaeval churches, as well as one of the oldest inns in the country. The Tabard at Stamford was a thriving business, and the family of Cecil's grandmother, Alice Dicons, had some interest in it, although, contrary to rumours intended to denigrate Cecil in later life, they were not the innkeepers.

The Tabard has been renamed the George, and is well worth a visit. Stamford school still exists too, although the buildings, which are dotted around the town, almost all post-date Cecil.

At the age of 14, the usual age, Cecil went to the College of St John the Evangelist, Cambridge (4). This College had been founded in the Will of Lady Margaret Beaufort, and so had associations for Cecil's family. During this period, he met and built relationships with some of the men who would influence him in religious matters and be politically associated with him throughout his career – John Cheke, Roger Ascham, Thomas Smith and Edmund Grindal were all either studying or teaching there. His friendship with John Cheke led on to affairs of the heart. To the intense disapproval of his father, he married Cheke's sister, Mary, although she died young, leaving Cecil with a baby son.

St John's College is still a functioning college of the university, and, in fact, is one of the largest. It can be visited between March and October between 10am and 5pm and during the winter between 10am and 3.30pm. A good proportion of the buildings are those that Cecil would have known – particularly the Great Gatehouse, completed in 1519 and sporting the arms of Lady Margaret – the Beaufort Portcullis supported by her heraldic beast, the Yale. The chapel is a gothic confection by Gilbert Scott, dating from the nineteenth century.

After his five years at St John's, Cecil went to study law at Gray's Inn (5). Again, the place itself is still an Inn of Court, but the buildings have been much altered. There are remnants that Cecil would have known as a student, in the Chapel and the Hall, although both have been extensively rebuilt since his time, the Hall as early as the 1550s, so it would look familiar to him.

In the early 1540s, with his marriage to Mildred, one of the daughters of the courtier, Sir Anthony Cooke, Cecil began to spend time in and around the King's court. It was not, however, until he was working for the Duke of Somerset, early in the reign of Edward VI that we have exact information on where he lived. At that time, he bought two houses in Canon Row, Westminster (6) from Lord Paget, for around £400 cash. This was not an insignificant amount of money, but there is no information as to how he raised it.

Cecil took his first trip out of the country in September 1549, when he travelled with the English army to Scotland. He was present at the Battle of Pinkie Cleugh, and afterwards, when the English marched on Edinburgh (7).

Returning from Scotland, Cecil continued to live at Canon Row, when in London, for at least ten years, but an aspiring courtier also needed a country home. In 1549, he became interested in property in Wimbledon, and discussed with Sir Robert Tyrwhitt, the possibility of acquiring the remainder of a sixty year lease of the Rectory of Wimbledon (8).

The lands in and around Wimbledon had been owned by the Abbey of Worcester, and, at the Dissolution of the Monasteries had transferred to the Crown. There were two parts to the estate – the Manor of Wimbledon, which included a manor house and was near modern Mortlake, and the Rectory, which included a Parsonage near the Church of St Mary's, Wimbledon.

The Rector had the right of presentation of rectors to the Church of St Mary's and curates to Mortlake and Putney. He also had the right to collect the tithes and either farm the glebe (church lands) himself, or lease it out. In return, the Rector had to maintain the three churches mentioned.

The Manor of Wimbledon had been granted to Thomas Cromwell, and then to Queen Katherine Parr. The Rectory had been returned to the Dean and Chapter of the new Cathedral at Worcester, who had leased it out, and it was the remainder of this lease that Cecil now acquired. He also acquired more land, north of what is now Worple Road in Wimbledon, stretching up towards the Common. He was fined 6d in 1555 for not maintaining his gate there properly.

During Edward's reign, Cecil spent the majority of his time at Canon Row, during Mary's sovereignty he spent more time at Wimbledon. It was in either of these places that the first four children of his marriage to Mildred were born – Frances, Anne, and two babies, both named William. Only Anne, born in Westminster, survived and the others are buried in St Mary's Church.

Living at Wimbledon with him were his wife, Mildred; his sister, Margaret, later Mrs Cave; Mildred's sister, Elizabeth, later Lady Hoby; his son, Thomas, and his two wards at the time, Arthur Hill and John Stanhope. When the Manor of Wimbledon was granted by Mary to Cardinal Pole, William became his steward for the land.

In late 1549, Cecil exchanged his comfortable quarters at Canon Row, for a stint in the Tower of London. As a gentleman prisoner of means, he would not have been kept in a dank cell, but in one of the better rooms. He would have had to pay for his own keep. His sojourn there was short, only about 5 weeks, but we can suppose he was glad to leave.

A far more enjoyable moment in a royal palace would have been on 5th September 1550, at Oatlands Palace (10) when he was given a place on the Privy Council as Secretary. Oatlands Palace, which was near the village of the same name in Surrey, has completely disappeared now – it was demolished under the Commonwealth in the 1650s. A single building on the estate, some distance from the palace, was developed into Oatlands House and parts of it are in the hotel currently on the site.

Another high point would have been at Hampton Court on 11th October 1551, when he was knighted.

It was at Ingatestone Hall, in Essex, the home of his fellow Secretary, Sir William Petre, that Cecil came to swear allegiance to Mary, after the failure of the attempt to replace her with Lady Jane Grey. Although the Queen pardoned him she did not immediately take him back into government service.

In the years when Cecil was not directly in government employ, he travelled around London and the nearby counties, visiting friends, such as the Hobys at Bisham, and his parents still in Stamford, on their property at Burghley, just south of the town. Cecil was a compulsive recorder of detail, and information exists about one of his trips to Burghley during this period, which he undertook in company with his servant, Thomas Cayworth.

The two left Wimbledon on the morning of Sunday, 2nd May, with four horses. Cecil crossed the river by the Wandsworth ferry, which delivered him close to Canon Row, whilst Cayforth had to detour up to Lambeth to take the animals across the Thames on the horse-ferry (hence the name Horseferry Road in South London today.) They slept at Canon Row that night, then, on the following day had dinner at Ware in Hertfordshire – probably about 11am, having covered 25 miles, followed by supper at Royston, a further 20 miles. We can infer from this that they followed the route of the modern A10. The next day they completed the full 50 miles on to Stamford, probably crossing westward to the Great North Road at Huntingdon.

Cecil remained in Stamford until 13th May, on which date he and Cayworth arrived in Huntingdon in time for dinner, and supped and slept at Royston. Dinner at Ware on 14th was followed by a long ride back into London, and a ferry crossing at Westminster, arriving at Stangate on the south side. From there, they probably followed what is now the A3 to arrive back in Wimbledon for bed. The whole journey cost 14s 5d on the outward trip, and 12s 5d to return.

There were two trips abroad during Mary's reign, the first, to Brussels to escort Cardinal Pole home, and the second, also to Brussels on government business, but followed up by independent travel to Antwerp and other places. During Mary's reign, Cecil also began his refurbishment of Burghley House at Stamford (3), which he inherited in 1553

We know that Cecil was at Hatfield in November 1558, when Elizabeth received the news of her half-sister's death. From that time he was in constant attendance on the Queen at the various royal palaces, Whitehall, Nonsuch, Richmond, Oatlands and others. In 1572 he was installed as the 356th Knight of the Order of the Garter, at St George's Chapel, Windsor Castle.

For domestic purposes, Cecil and his family had outgrown Wimbledon, which was passed to his son, Thomas. Instead, Cecil developed a grand new property in the Strand. Cecil House (14) was situated more or less opposite where the Savoy Theatre is today. He lavished time and money on it, and it was here that he died in 1598.

But even Cecil House and Burghley House did not satisfy Cecil's architectural passions. He created the most beautiful of all of the Elizabeth Prodigy houses at Theobalds, near Cheshunt, on the northern fringes of London. Nothing remains of it today – another palace pulled down during the Commonwealth.

For all Cecil's ties to London, when he died, he chose to go home to Stamford. Following his death on 4th August, 1598, at Cecil House, he began his last journey. He was transported to Westminster Abbey where over five hundred people attended his funeral. Then, following his orders, his cortege which consisted of only twelve men, accompanied the black draped coach containing the coffin the 100 miles to Stamford. At each resting place the poor of the parish were to be given 40s. He was entombed next to the memorial he had built for his parents in the church of St Martin Without, a thirteenth century church on the west of Stamford, about a mile from Burghley. There he rests, alone in his sumptuous monument, awaiting the resurrection and that final passage he so firmly believed in.

Key to Map

1. Bourne, Lincolnshire

2. Grantham – School

3. Stamford – School & Church, Burghley House

4. St John's College, Cambridge

5. Gray's Inn, London

6. Canon's Row, London

7. Edinburgh

8. Wimbledon Rectory & Church, London

9. Tower of London

10. Oatlands Palace, Surrey

11. Hampton Court Palace, Greater London

12. Ingatestone Hall, Essex

13. Windsor Castle

14. Cecil House, London

15. Theobalds, near Cheshunt (Greater London)

Chapter 19: Book Review

William Cecil has been the subject of many biographies over time, from the early ones written by members of his staff, to the Victorian hagiographies praising a great Protestant Statesman. Amongst modern works, the most comprehensive is that of Stephen Alford which, although not exhaustive on every topic, is a work of considerable scope.

Burghley: William Cecil at the Court of Elizabeth I

Author: Stephen Alford

Publisher: Yale University Press

In a nutshell A vast, detailed study of Elizabeth I's chief minister. William Cecil, Lord Burghley, emerges as a dedicated public servant, who believed totally in his destiny to protect Elizabeth and the Protestant state – with or without her agreement.

Stephen Alford is a Fellow of King's College, Cambridge, and has made a life-long study of the politicians of Elizabeth's court. His profound knowledge of the minute detail of every aspect of Burghley's long life and service pervade every page.

Many books portray Elizabeth and Cecil as two sides of the same coin – his role being to carry out her policy, but Alford suggests a rather different picture, perhaps supporting some of the anti-Cecil rhetoric of the day that saw him as too powerful, and tending to usurp the Queen's authority. There is no doubt that Alford's Cecil would have rejected such a view. He was devoted to the Queen's cause, it was just that he sometimes knew her interests, and those of her country, better than she did.

Alford identifies a number of occasions when Burghley, whilst ostensibly carrying out the Queen's policy, in fact, was attempting to subvert it through manipulating Parliament. In particular he cites the drafting of the petition put forward in 1566 for the Queen's marriage, which, he identifies was Cecil's brain-child, unbeknownst to the Queen, even whilst he was replying on her behalf with one of her famous '*answers answerless*'.

One of the underlying themes of the book is Cecil's obsession with the threat posed by Mary, Queen of Scots. How much of this threat he created through his own policy is left as the unanswered question – for who can know? But a case could certainly be made that his relentless undermining of her position in Scotland, and his later covering up of the forgeries in the Casket Letters, were all steps on his ultimate goal – her death.

Burghley's personality comes out well in Alford's writing – his tirelessness, his frequent ill health, his obsessive-compulsive need to control everything, from insisting on writing almost all his letters himself, to his minute directions to his son's guardian in Paris, to prevent young Thomas sitting up late over supper.

Cecil's family was important to him. His first marriage, to Mary Cheke, is over in a couple of paragraphs, but his forty-two year marriage to Mildred Cooke and their close relationship is interwoven into the story, together with his love and concern for his daughter, Anne, Countess of Oxford. Nevertheless, he was an exacting parent, and his relationship with his elder son was poor.

A man of omnivorous knowledge and interests, Alford brings out Cecil's other interests, which he pursued whenever he had leisure – architecture, gardening, map and book collecting.

Areas that could have been covered in more depth might have been Burghley's relationships with the Puritans, his views on the '*prophesying*' debate and the imprisonment of Grindal.

Another area that Alford does not explore at all (perhaps because he perceives it to be baseless sensation-mongering, which is probably true) is the hint in other studies of the period that Cecil might have had a hand in the death of Lord Robert Dudley's wife, Amy Robsart.

All in all, however, a book that is difficult to fault for its combination of depth and breadth.

Bibliography

Calendar of State Papers: Domestic Series: Edward VI, 1547-1553. United Kingdom: Stationery Office Books.

Calendar of State Papers: Domestic: Mary I 1553-1558. London: Public Record Office.

Calendar of State Papers Simancas, British History Online (HMSO, 1892) Hume, Martin A S, ed.,

Calendar of State Papers: Venice <http://www.british-history.ac.uk/cal-state-papers/venice/vol2/vii-lxi> [accessed 7 October 2015]

Cecil Papers, http://www.british-history.ac.uk/cal-cecil-papers (Accessed: 7 September 2015)

Letters and Papers, Foreign and Domestic, of the Reign of Henry VIII: Preserved in the Public Record Office, the British Museum, and Elsewhere in England (United Kingdom: British History Online, 2014) https://www.british-history.ac.uk/letters-papers-hen8/ Brewer, John Sherren, and James Gairdner,

Alford, Stephen, *Burghley: William Cecil at the Court of Elizabeth I* (London: Yale University Press, 2008)

Charlton, W B, *Burghley* (Stamford, Lincs: W. Langley, 1847)

Childs, Jessie, *God's Traitors: Terror and Faith in Elizabethan England* (United States: Oxford University Press, USA, 2014)

Danner, Bruce, *Edmund Spenser's War on Lord Burghley* (Houndmills, Basingstoke, Hampshire: Palgrave Macmillan, 2011)

De Lisle, Leanda, *Tudor: The Family Story* (United Kingdom: Chatto & Windus, 2013)

De Lisle, Leanda, *The Sisters Who Would Be Queen the Tragedy of Mary, Katherine, & Lady Jane Grey* (Glasgow: HarperCollins e-books, 2008)

Doran, S. *The Tudor Chronicles.* (London: Quercus Publishing Plc, 2008)

Doran, S. *Elizabeth I and her Circle* 1st edn. (Oxford: OUP, 2015)

Fletcher, A. and Vernon, L. (1973) *Tudor Rebellions (Seminar Studies in History).* 2nd edn. Harlow: Longman.

Foxe, John, *The Acts and Monuments of John Foxe: A New and Complete Edition: With a Preliminary Dissertation by the Rev. George Townsend* (London: R.R. Seeley and W. Burnside, 1837)

Guy, John, *Elizabeth and Cecil,* <http://www.tudors.org/undergraduate/elizabeth-and-cecil/> [accessed 6 September 2015]

Higham, C S S, *Wimbledon Manor House under the Cecils* (Longmans Green & Co. Ltd, 1962)

Hoby, Sir Thomas, *The Travels and Life of Sir Thomas Hoby Kt of Bisham Abbey, Written by Himself 1547 - 1564*, ed. by Edgar Powell (London: Royal Historical Society, 1902)

Holinshed, Raphael, *Holinshed's Chronicles of England, Scotland & Ireland* (United Kingdom: AMS Press, 1997)

Ives, Eric, *Lady Jane Grey: A Tudor Mystery*, 1st edn (United Kingdom: Wiley-Blackwell (an imprint of John Wiley & Sons Ltd), 2012)

Keith, Robert: *History of the Affairs of Church and State in Scotland from the Beginning of the Reformation to the Year 1568* (Edinburgh: Spottiswoode, 1844),

Lemon, Robert, ed., *Calendar of State Papers: Domestic Series: Edward, Mary and Elizabeth,* British History Online (London: HMSO, 1856)

Lettenhove, Kervyn de, ed., *Relations Politiques Des Pays-Bas et d'Angleterre* (Brussels: L'Academie Royale de Belgique, 1882)

Lindsay of Pitscottie, Robert, *Pitscottie's Chronicles of Scotland,* ed. by Ae. J. G Mackay (Edinburgh: Blackwood for the Society, 1911)

Marshall, Rosalind K, *John Knox* (Edinburgh: Birlinn, 2008)

Morse H., *Select Documents Of English Constitutional History,* ed. by George Burton Adams and Morse H Stephens (United States: Kessinger Publishing, 2007)

Porter, Linda, *Crown of Thistles: The Fatal Inheritance of Mary Queen of Scots* (United Kingdom: Macmillan, 2013)

Reid, Stuart, *Battles of the Scottish Lowlands* (Barnsley: Pen & Sword Military, 2004)

Ritchie, P. E. (2002) *Mary of Guise in Scotland, 1548-1560: A Political Study.* United Kingdom: Tuckwell Press.

Ross, Josephine, *Suitors to the Queen: The Men in the Life of Elizabeth I of England,* 1st edn (New York: Coward, McCann & Geoghegan, 1975)

Sidney, Philip, *'Jane the Quene': Being Some Account of the Life and Literary Remains of Lady Jane Dudley, Commonly Called Lady Jane Grey* (London: Swann, Sonneschein and Co., 1900)

Simms, Brendan, *Europe: The Struggle for Supremacy, from 1453 to the Present* (United States: Basic Books, 2014)

Skelton, R A, and John Summerson, *A Description of Maps and Architectural Drawings in the Collection Made by William Cecil, First Baron Burghley, Now at Hatfield House* (Oxford: Oxford Press, 1971)

Strickland, A. and Strickland, E. (2011) *Lives of the Queens of England from the Norman Conquest: Volume 3 & 4*. United Kingdom: Cambridge University Press (Virtual Publishing).

Strype, John, *Annals of the Reformation and Establishment of Religion and Other Various Occurrences in the Church of England Etc.* (Oxford: Clarendon Press, 1824),

Weir, Alison, *Elizabeth, the Queen,* Kindle (London: Random House UK, 2009)

Whitelock, Anna, *Elizabeth's Bedfellows*, Kindle (London: Bloomsbury Publishing PLC, 2013)

Whitelock, A. (2010) *Mary Tudor: princess, bastard, queen.* 1st edn. New York: Random House Publishing Group.

Williams, Neville, *The Life and Times of Elizabeth I* (New York: Welcome Rain Publishers, 1998)

Wimbledon Common Committee, ed., *Extracts from the Court Rolls of the Manor of Wimbledon from Edward IV to AD 1864* (London: Wyman and Sons, 1866)

www.tudortimes.co.uk

www.ingramcontent.com/pod-product-compliance
Lightning Source LLC
Chambersburg PA
CBHW021210020426
42331CB00003B/292